— SHAKESPEARE'S —

KING LEAR

A GRAPHIC NOVEL

Adapted by

Steve Barlow and Steve Skidmore

Illustrated by Juan Calle

W
FRANKLIN WATTS
LONDON•SYDNEY

FRANKLIN WATTS
FIRST PUBLISHED IN GREAT BRITAIN IN 2025
BY HODDER AND STOUGHTON

CREDITS:
EDITOR: GRACE GLENDINNING
DESIGNER: CATHRYN GILBERT
COVER AND INTERIOR ILLUSTRATION: JUAN CALLE
COLOUR: LUIS SUAREZ AND SANTIAGO CALLE (LIBERUM DONUM)
ADDITIONAL ILLUSTRATION: JASON MILLET AND EDU RUBIO FOR THE ART ON PAGES 4--5, 106--107, 112

PICTURE CREDITS: PAGE 109 COLIN WATERS / ALAMY STOCK PHOTO
EVERY ATTEMPT HAS BEEN MADE TO CLEAR COPYRIGHT. SHOULD THERE BE ANY INADVERTENT OMISSION PLEASE APPLY TO THE PUBLISHER FOR RECTIFICATION.

HB ISBN: 978 1 4451 9026 6
PB ISBN: 978 1 4451 9028 0
EB ISBN: 978 1 4451 9027 3

PRINTED IN CHINA

FRANKLIN WATTS
AN IMPRINT OF
HACHETTE CHILDREN'S GROUP
PART OF HODDER AND STOUGHTON
CARMELITE HOUSE
50 VICTORIA EMBANKMENT
LONDON EC4Y 0DZ

AN HACHETTE UK COMPANY
WWW.HACHETTE.CO.UK
WWW.HACHETTECHILDRENS.CO.UK

WARNING: *King Lear* contains some difficult discussions and images of violence, murder and suicide, which may be triggering and distressing to some readers. Please only read when you feel able to do so.

THE AUTHORISED REPRESENTATIVE IN THE EEA IS HACHETTE IRELAND, 8 CASTLECOURT CENTRE, DUBLIN 15, D15 XTP3, IRELAND (EMAIL: INFO@HBGI.IE)

CONTENTS

William Shakespeare:

The Man, the Actor, the Author

William Shakespeare is considered to be one of the greatest writers who ever lived.

He was born in the market town of Stratford-upon-Avon in Warwickshire, England in 1564 and died there in 1616.

Shakespeare is usually referred to as an Elizabethan playwright but he actually lived during the reign of two monarchs: Elizabeth I and James I. When Elizabeth died in 1603, James, who was already King of Scotland, took over the English throne.

During Shakespeare's lifetime, he wrote nearly 40 plays and over 150 poems (mainly sonnets). He was also an actor, a very successful businessman and owned valuable buildings and land in London and Stratford.

His parents were John Shakespeare, a glove-maker and Stratford council official, and Mary Arden, who was the daughter of a wealthy local farmer. As the child of a reasonably well-off family, William attended the local grammar school, where he would have studied Latin and Greek as well as English literature and history.

In 1582, at the age of 18, he married Anne Hathaway. They had three children but by 1587, Shakespeare had left his wife and children in Stratford and moved to London. He joined an acting company and, by the early 1590s, was writing his own plays, becoming well known and successful in the world of London theatre.

In 1594, Shakespeare joined a new acting company, The Lord Chamberlain's Men, with his friend, the actor Richard Burbage. He would spend the rest of his life writing plays to be performed by this company and even became a part-owner of The Globe Theatre, which was built in 1599. This company was so successful that when King James came to the throne, he became their sponsor and their name was changed to The King's Men.

From 1610, Shakespeare began to spend more time in Stratford. He died on 23rd April, 1616. In the years following Shakespeare's death, two of his friends, John Heminge and Henry Condell, collected manuscripts and copies of his plays. They were printed in 1623 in an edition known as *The First Folio*. This collection of tragedies, comedies and historical plays helped to establish Shakespeare as a great playwright – possibly the greatest the world has ever known.

Another friend, the playwright Ben Jonson, said that Shakespeare's plays would prove to be "not of an age, but for all time".

Jonson was right. Shakespeare's plays have been translated into every major language and are performed across the world. They have also been turned into films, TV series, musicals, ballets and graphic novels!

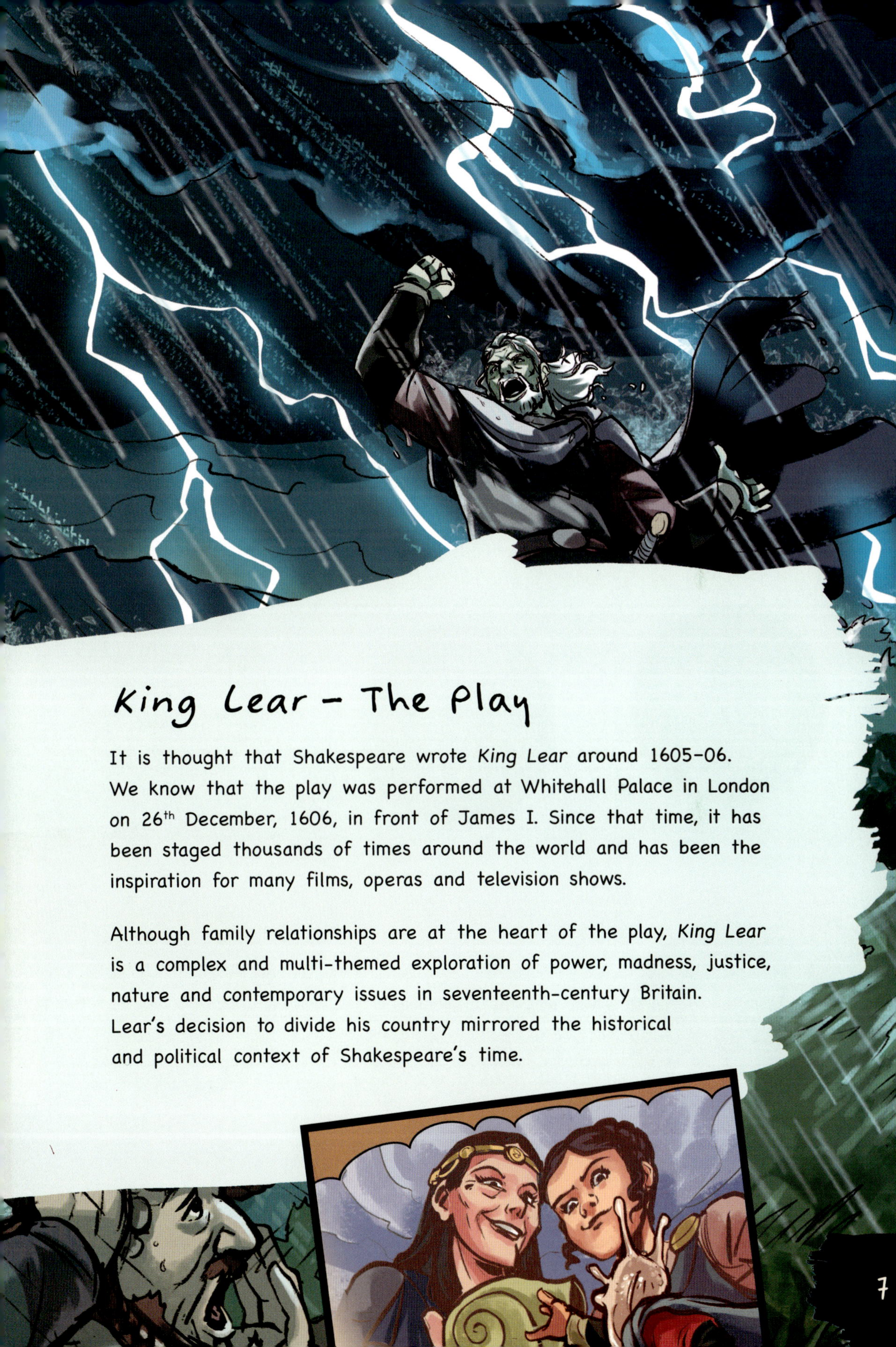

King Lear – The Play

It is thought that Shakespeare wrote *King Lear* around 1605–06. We know that the play was performed at Whitehall Palace in London on 26th December, 1606, in front of James I. Since that time, it has been staged thousands of times around the world and has been the inspiration for many films, operas and television shows.

Although family relationships are at the heart of the play, *King Lear* is a complex and multi-themed exploration of power, madness, justice, nature and contemporary issues in seventeenth-century Britain. Lear's decision to divide his country mirrored the historical and political context of Shakespeare's time.

In 1603, King James VI of Scotland had ascended the throne of England to become James I of England. He wished to unite the kingdoms peacefully. The English Parliament were against this – the Act of Union did not take place for another hundred years (1707). In the play, Shakespeare's audience sees for themselves the dangerous consequences of Lear's 'carving up' of Britain: civil war and bloodshed.

Many people argue that *King Lear* is Shakespeare's greatest play. The Romantic poet, Percy Bysshe Shelley, called it, "the most perfect specimen of the dramatic art existing in the world". In contrast, some notable critics have found it, "painful and disgusting" and, "although great literature [...] essentially impossible to be represented on a stage". Such opposing views are the mark of what great literature can do: make us think, question and consider. *King Lear* is a play that certainly achieves this.

It also has many of Shakespeare's most memorable lines.

"Nothing will come of nothing. Speak again."
Lear Act 1 Scene 1

"Thou shouldst not have been old till thou hadst been wise."
Fool Act 1 Scene 5

"I am a man more sinned against than sinning."
Lear Act 3 Scene 2

"When we are born, we cry that we are come To this great stage of fools."
Lear Act 4 Scene 5

"As flies to wanton boys are we to th' gods;
They kill us for their sport."
Gloucester Act 4 Scene 1

"Blow, winds, and crack your cheeks! Rage, blow,
You cataracts and hurricanoes, spout
Till you have drenched our steeples, drowned the cocks!"
Lear Act 3 Scene 2

KING LEAR
BRITAIN, MANY HUNDREDS OF YEARS AGO
LEAR IS THE KING OF ANCIENT BRITAIN. HE IS NEARING THE END OF HIS LIFE AND WISHES TO DIVIDE HIS KINGDOM EQUALLY AMONG HIS THREE DAUGHTERS. HE HAS CALLED HIS FAMILY AND NOBLES TOGETHER TO ANNOUNCE HIS DECISION ABOUT WHICH DAUGHTER WILL GET WHICH PORTION OF THE COUNTRY.
OBSERVE HOW HIS CHILDREN RECEIVE THIS NEWS...
Lear's Britain
BRITAIN
London
Dover

List Of Main Characters

Dramatis Personae

The Royal House Of Britain

GONERIL

Lear's eldest daughter

LEAR

King of Britain

REGAN

Lear's middle daughter

DUKE OF ALBANY

Goneril's husband

CORDELIA

Lear's youngest daughter

DUKE OF CORNWALL

Regan's husband

The Gloucester Family

EDGAR

Gloucester's eldest son and heir (later disguised as POOR TOM)

EARL OF GLOUCESTER

EDMUND

Gloucester's illegitimate son

Other Main Characters

EARL OF KENT

A loyal servant of Lear, later disguised as CAIUS

FOOL

A servant of Lear

KING OF FRANCE

Suitor and later husband to Cordelia

DUKE OF BURGUNDY

Suitor to Cordelia

OSWALD

Goneril's steward

DOCTOR

OLD MAN

Gloucester's tenant

Others

CURAN
CAPTAIN
HERALD
SERVANTS
GENTLEMEN

ACT 1
KING LEAR'S COURT, BRITAIN
Is this your son, my Lord Gloucester?
Yes, I am Edmund's father, although he was not conceived by my wife! I also have a legitimate son, Edgar. But I love both sons equally. Edmund, this is Lord Kent. He is my friend.
I am pleased to meet you, my Lord.
I look forward to getting to know you better.
Edmund has been abroad for nine years and leaves again very soon.
The King is coming!

Gloucester, bring in the Lords of France and Burgundy, while I reveal the real reason I have brought you all here.
As I am getting older and wish for an easier life, I have divided my Kingdom into three parts. My three daughters will each receive a part.
Albany and Cornwall, you will know today what your wives will own, so that there will be no conflict between you after I'm dead.
Cordelia, The King of France and the Duke of Burgundy are rivals for your hand in marriage, and they too will soon know what your dowry will be.
So, my daughters. Which one of you will say that you love me the most? The one that does so will receive the greatest reward! Goneril, my eldest, speak first!

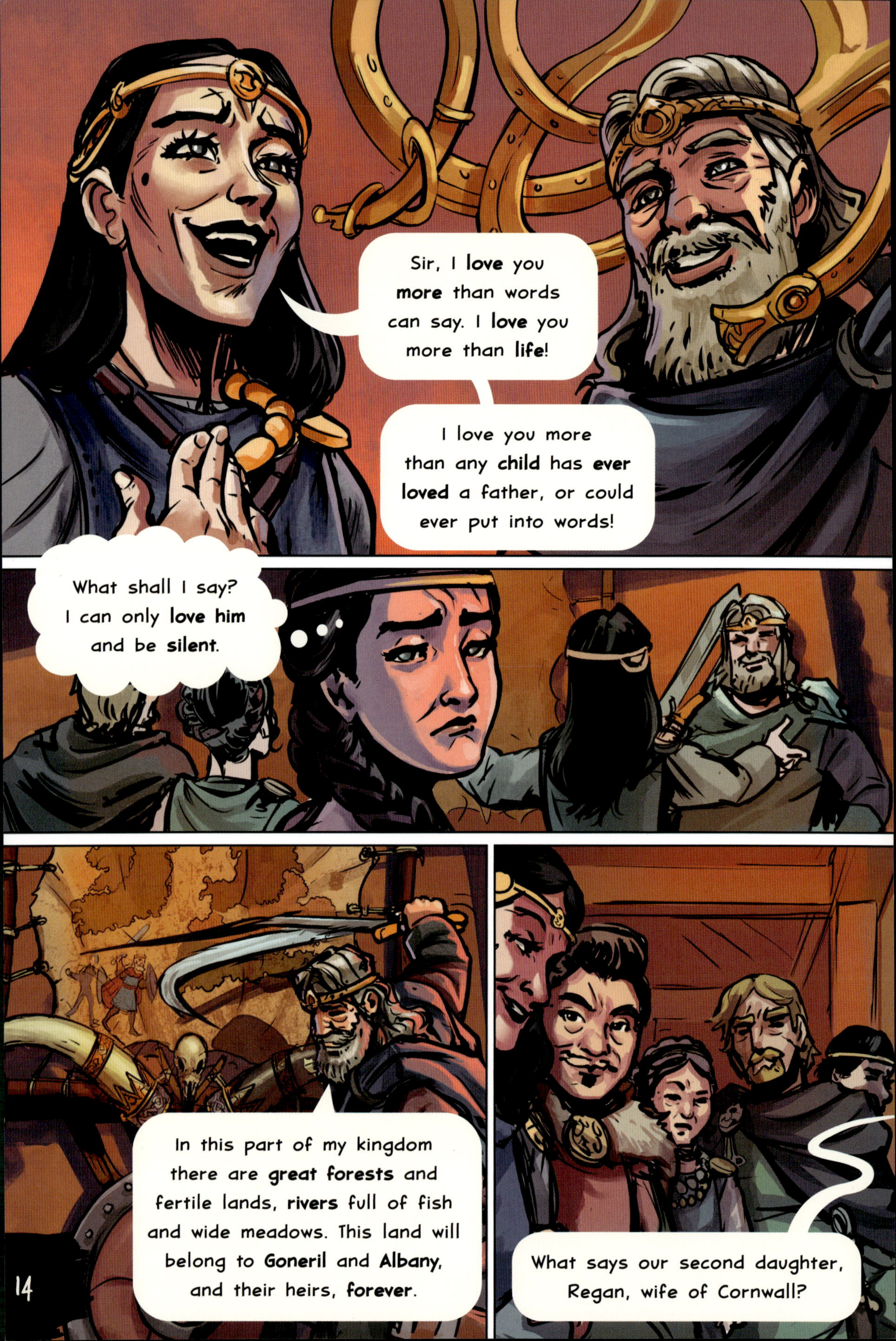

Sir, I **love** you **more** than words can say. I **love** you more than **life**!

I love you more than any **child** has **ever** **loved** a father, or could ever put into words!

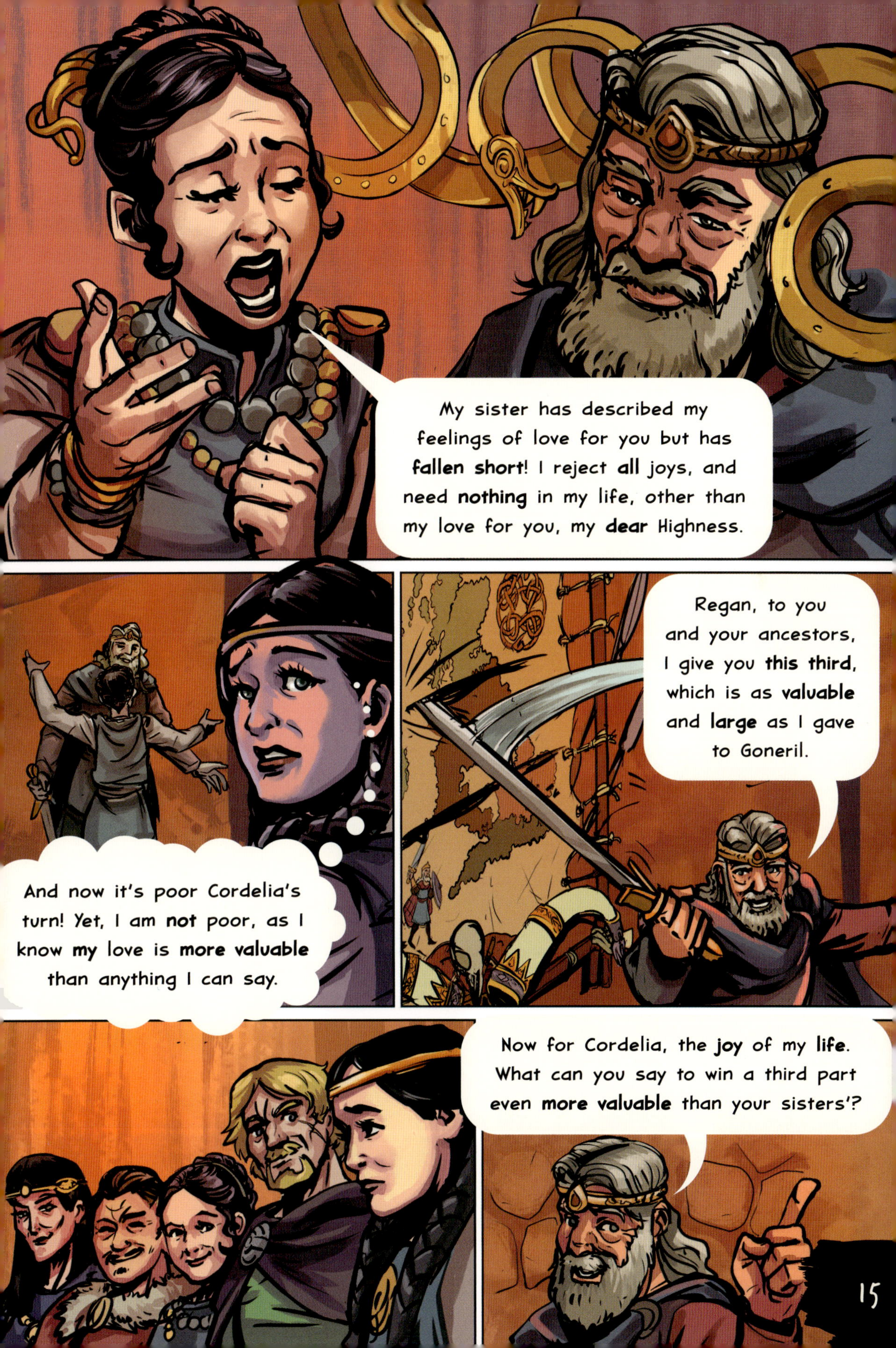

My sister has described my feelings of love for you but has **fallen short**! I reject **all** joys, and need **nothing** in my life, other than my love for you, my **dear** Highness.

Nothing, my Lord.
Nothing?
Nothing.
Nothing will come of nothing. Speak again.
I am unlucky, for I cannot put my heart's **feelings** into **words**. I love your majesty as a **child** should love her **father**, **no more**, **no less**.
!?!!
What! Change what you are saying, or it will **damage** your future.
You are my father. You have brought me up and loved me, and so I **return** those duties. I truly **love** and **honour** you.
But why do my sisters say they love **only you**? They have husbands. Don't they love them too? When I am married, my husband will **also** have my love and honour.

Do you really mean this?
Yes, my Lord.
So young and so heartless?
So young, my Lord, and true.
Very well! Truth will be your only inheritance! I disown you as my daughter. I am no longer your father!
But, sir ...
Peace, Kent! Do not come between the dragon and his anger.
I loved her most! But now ...!
Get out of my sight, Cordelia! I never want to see you again!
Cornwall and Albany, you and your wives can divide her third of the kingdom between yourselves.
I will keep the title of King, but you will jointly hold the power.
I will live a month with one of you and the next month with the other. All I want is one hundred knights to serve me.

I give you this crown to confirm this all.
Royal Lear, whom I have served and loved ...
Beware, Kent. I am like a drawn bow, ready to snap.
I will be rude when Lear goes mad!
I must speak out at your foolish decision. Cordelia loves you just as much as the other two do.
Kent, be silent if you want to live!
I am not afraid to lose my life to protect you. Take back your crown or I will continue to say that what you are doing is evil to my last breath!
Hear me, traitor! You will be punished!
You have five days to pack what goods you need to survive and on the sixth you are banished from this kingdom! If you are found here after that time, you will die. Go!

Farewell, King. **Freedom**, too, is banished from your land. Cordelia, I hope the gods protect you. Goneril, Regan, I hope your grand words achieve great results. Farewell, all.

The rulers of Burgundy and France, my Lord.

You both want Cordelia's hand in marriage. Burgundy, what is the **least** you will take for a dowry?
No more than you have already offered, your Majesty. Will you now offer **less**?

Her **value** has **fallen**! If you like what you see, take it. But her only dowry is my **curse**. Take her or leave her.

I cannot choose her in these circumstances.
Then leave her - she's not worth anything.

Great King, I would not **insult** you by giving you something I **hate**. Find someone else to marry, not this **wretch**.

This is most strange. She was your **favourite**. She must have committed a terrible crime against you to deserve such **hatred**. I cannot believe she is capable of such a deed.

Your Majesty, my only fault is that I **do not** seek fortune and don't have a **glib** way with words. And I am glad of this, although it has **lost** me your love.

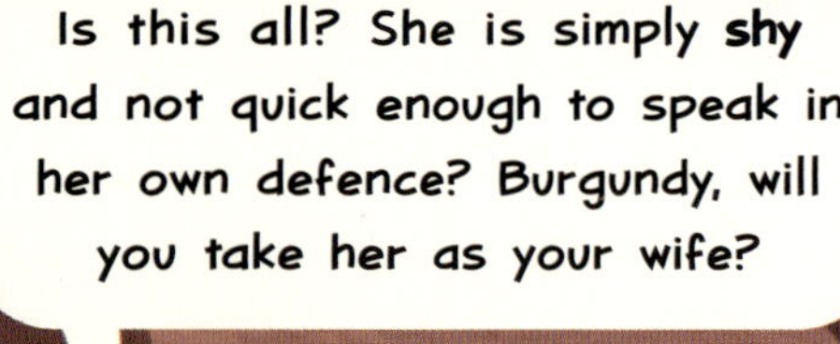

It would have been better that you had **not been born**, than **displeased** me so.

Is this all? She is simply **shy** and not quick enough to speak in her own defence? Burgundy, will you take her as your wife?

Not without the **land** that was offered.

Then **I will** take you. King, the daughter you have rejected will be my **Queen** of France. Cordelia, you will find a **better** home with me than here.

She's **yours**, France. She is **no longer** my daughter and I **never** wish to see her again.

Sisters, I **know** what you **truly** are. Take good care of our father. Farewell.
Don't tell us what to do.
You look after your Lord, who has only taken you as an act of charity.
Time will tell what you are **really** planning, and **truth** will be revealed.
Come away, my fair Cordelia.
Our father is growing old and moody. Banishing his beloved Cordelia shows his **bad** judgement.
He's **always** been rash, but he's growing even more impulsive and bad-tempered in his old age.
His unpredictable outbursts will **continue**.
We need a plan.
If he continues to use his authority like this, it will do us no good. We **must** do something...

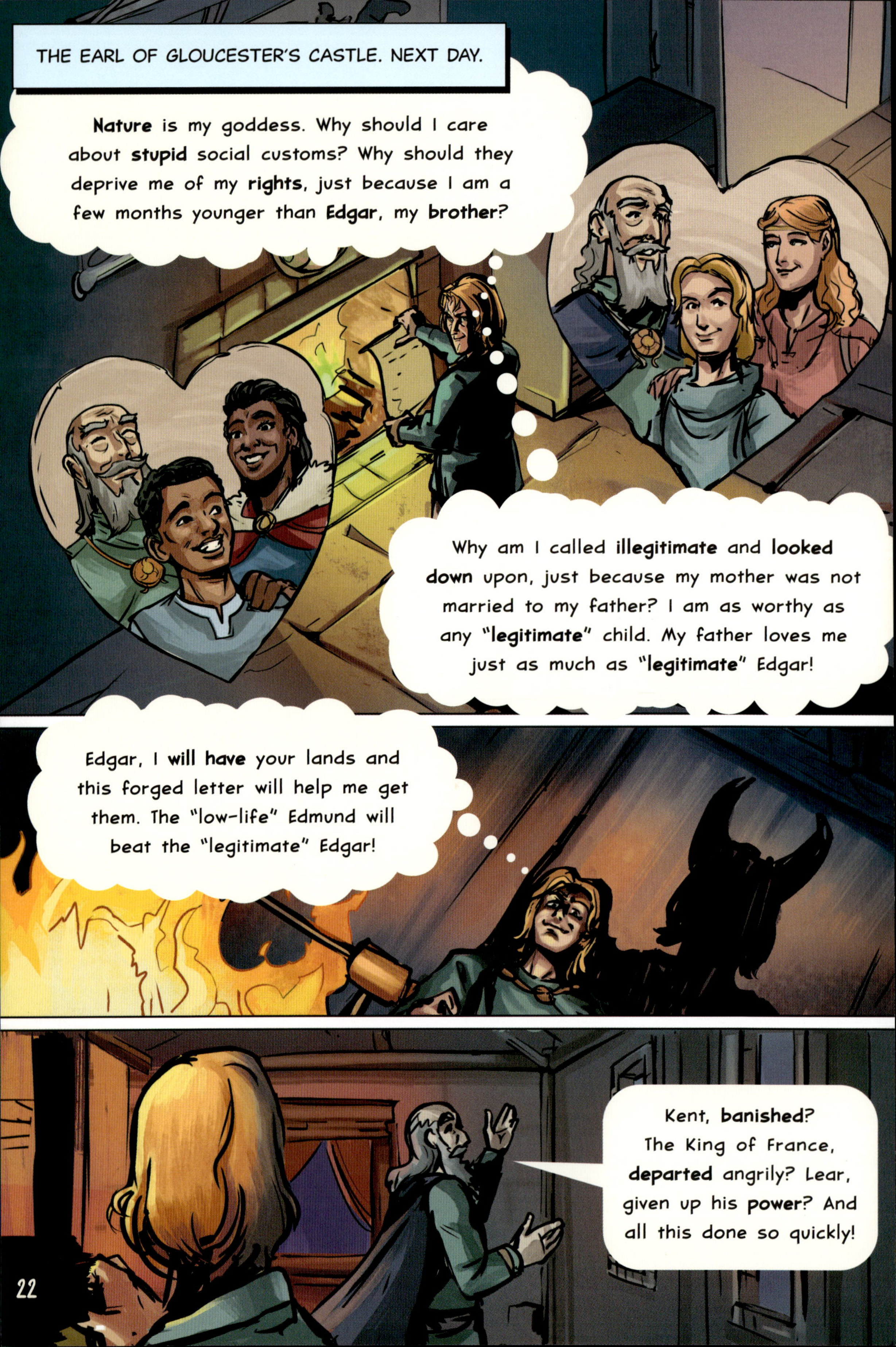

THE EARL OF GLOUCESTER'S CASTLE. NEXT DAY.

Nature is my goddess. Why should I care about **stupid** social customs? Why should they deprive me of my **rights**, just because I am a few months younger than **Edgar**, my **brother**?

Why am I called **illegitimate** and **looked down** upon, just because my mother was not married to my father? I am as worthy as any "**legitimate**" child. My father loves me just as much as "**legitimate**" Edgar!

Edgar, I **will have** your lands and this forged letter will help me get them. The "low-life" Edmund will beat the "legitimate" Edgar!

It is a letter from Edgar, but I haven't finished reading it yet. What I **have** read, you **won't like**.

Give me the letter.

The contents are **not good**! I'm sure my brother only wrote it to test my virtue.

And is this **your brother's** handwriting?
It is, but I'm sure he **didn't mean** what he wrote. **Although**... I **have** heard him say that when fathers grow old, **the sons** should look after the money.

Evil **villain**! Find and arrest him! Where **is** he?

I don't know, but I think it best to find out what he meant first. By acting rashly, you could **damage** your reputation and **lose** his loyalty!

I'm sure he has only written this to test my love for you. I'll arrange a meeting with him. *You* can hide and listen in to the conversation.

He cannot be such a monster. Find out what he is **truly** thinking. I would give up **everything** to find out the truth.
Do what is best, but do it **carefully**, Edmund.
I will, sir.
And here he comes. Right on cue!

Brother. When did you last see my father?
Just last night.
Did he seem **displeased** with you?
Not at all.

Try to think how you might have **offended** him. And stay away from him. He is **raging** against you and could do you harm!
Some villain has told lies about me.
That's my fear, too. Come with me to my rooms. I'll arrange a meeting with you and Father when he has calmed down.

Here is my key. If you **do** leave the room, make sure you're armed.
Armed?
I wouldn't be honest if I said that our father has **any** good intentions towards you. I'm doing **everything** to help you. Go now.

A **gullible** father and a brother so honest that he **cannot** see **evil** in anyone. If I can't have his lands by **birthright**, I'll get them by **cunning**.

ALBANY AND GONERIL'S CASTLE
TWO WEEKS LATER ...

Oswald, did my father strike one of my servants for telling off his fool?

Ay, madam.

He **offends** me every hour of every day! And he loses his temper, creating trouble for **everyone**!

His knights are growing **riotous**, and he **criticises** us **all the time**! I'm fed up.

I will not speak with him when he returns from hunting. Tell him I'm sick! And don't bother looking after him. I **want** to make an issue out of it.

I hear his hunting horns. He is returning, ma'am.

Be **lazy and neglectful** around him and his knights! If he doesn't like it, he can go and live with my sister. She feels as I do about him. I'll write to her and tell her to do **exactly** what I'm doing.

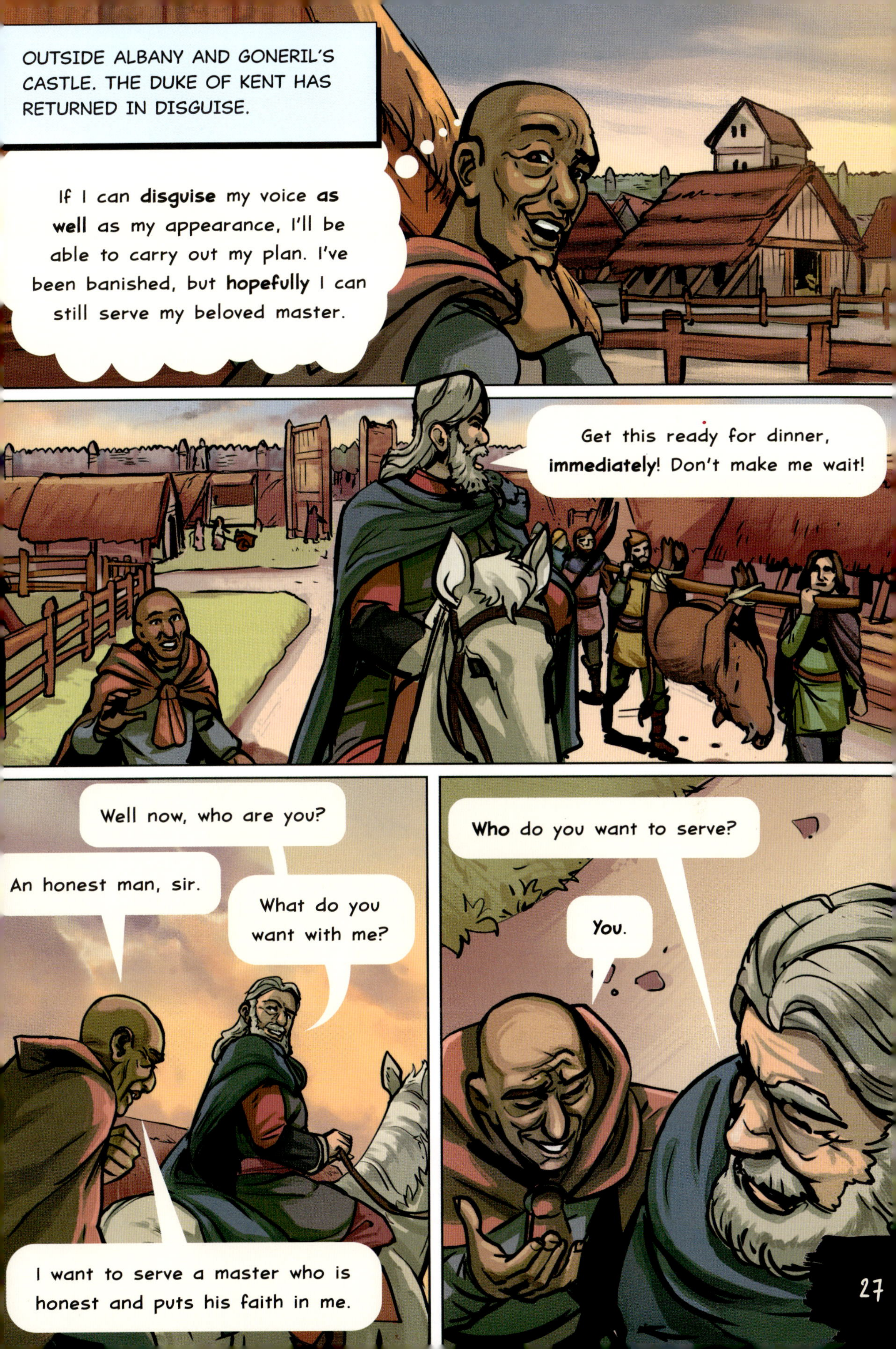

OUTSIDE ALBANY AND GONERIL'S CASTLE. THE DUKE OF KENT HAS RETURNED IN DISGUISE.

If I can **disguise** my voice **as well** as my appearance, I'll be able to carry out my plan. I've been banished, but **hopefully** I can still serve my beloved master.

Get this ready for dinner, **immediately**! Don't make me wait!

Do you know me, fellow?
No, sir, but you have **something** in your face that makes me want to call you master.
What's that?
Authority.
What services can you perform?
I can do **anything** an ordinary man can do, and above all, I'm hard-working.
Follow me! And if I still like you after dinner...
...you can stay!
Dinnertime! Someone get my fool!
You sir, Where's my daughter?
Sorry, I am busy.
What?! Do you know who I am?
My Lady's father.
"My Lady's father!" How **dare** you!
You **peasant**! You **worthless** dog!

I'll not be struck!
Or tripped, you dirty football player!
I'll teach you to respect your betters! Get up and get out!
Oh, you are serving me well!
Here's my clever fool! How are you?
How now, Uncle! I wish I had two hats and two daughters.
Why?
I'd give them everything and keep the fool's hats for myself.
Be careful, sir. You can be whipped!
If you give me an egg, I can break the egg, eat the middle and give you two crowns. When you divided your gold crown and gave away both parts, you didn't have much wit in your bald crown. If anyone thinks I'm lying, then let him be whipped!

I will have you whipped for lying!
You and your daughters are **alike**. They'll have me whipped for telling the **truth** and you'll have me whipped for **lying** ... and sometimes I'm whipped for **keeping quiet**!
!!!
I'd rather be **anything** but a fool, but I **wouldn't** want to be you, Uncle. You've sliced your head in two and left **nothing** in the middle. I am a fool, **you** are nothing!
Here's one of your daughters ...
She looks in a mood! I'm going to say nothing.
How now, daughter? **Why** do you frown?
This fool and all of your followers are **unruly** and **offensive**. I thought you'd do something about it, but I now think that you **encourage** them!
If you **don't** punish them, **you** will have to pay for this – for the **good** of the kingdom.

Are you my daughter?

I just wish you would **stop acting** so **foolishly**. Return to your true wise self.

Even a fool knows when everything is the wrong way round, and the cart is pulling the horse.

It is my request that you **reduce** their number. If you don't, **I'll** do it myself.

Darkness and **devils**! Saddle my horses! Call my knights! I'll not trouble you anymore. You're **no child of mine**! You'll **regret** this, but by then it will be **too late**!
I still have one true daughter left.
You **hateful** vulture. My knights are men of excellent qualities.

Cordelia's small flaw has broken my body and sucked the love out of me.
Oh, Lear, Lear, Lear!

Let me beat at this gate that let **foolishness** in and **wisdom out**!

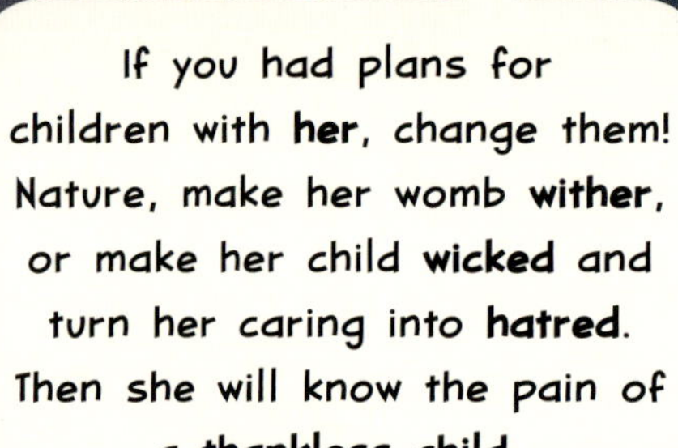
My Lord, what has **upset** you?
If you had plans for children with **her**, change them! Nature, make her womb **wither**, or make her child **wicked** and turn her caring into **hatred**. Then she will know the pain of a **thankless child**.

I am **ashamed** that you have the power to make me cry. If I cry again, I'll rip out my eyes!
When Regan hears what you've done, she'll **rip open** your face with her fingernails. Then I'll have my power back!

Away, away!
Goneril, you know I love you but ...
Hold your peace.
Why should he keep a hundred knights? What if he turns them against us?
You might be worrying unduly.
It's better to get rid of dangers before they can hurt you.
I've written to Regan and told her of his behaviour. I'm sure she won't want him and his hundred knights in her house. Oswald is taking the letter.
My Lord, I don't condemn your mild and gentle ways, but you are showing a lack of wisdom towards him.
All right, all right. Let's see what happens.

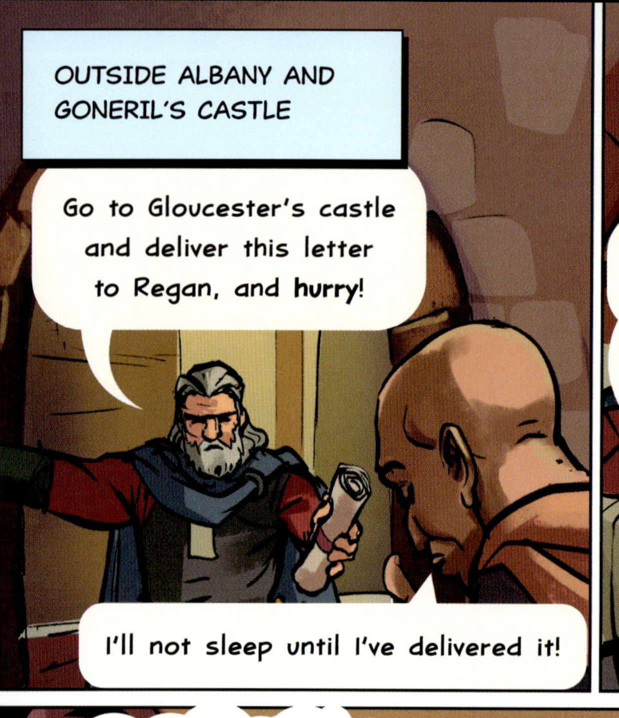

I was a **kind father**! I could have taken back my kingdom by force! What ingratitude.

If you were my fool, Uncle, I'd have you beaten for getting old before you had also **grown wise**.

Oh, let me not be mad, **not mad**, sweet Heaven! Keep me **sane**! I **don't** want to go **mad**!

ACT 2
LATER THAT NIGHT, IN THE GREAT HALL OF GLOUCESTER'S CASTLE.
I have told your father that the Duke of Cornwall and Regan will be staying here tonight.
Why is that, Curan?
I don't know. But there are rumours that there will be **a war** between Cornwall and Albany. I'm sure you will hear more of this. Farewell, sir.
The Duke – here tonight! Excellent! My father is ready to **arrest Edgar** and I have **one more** difficult thing to do. I need swift action and good fortune to succeed.
Brother, someone has betrayed your hiding place. Have you criticised the Duke of Cornwall? He's coming here **tonight**, with Regan.
Have you said anything against Cornwall's enemy, The Duke of Albany?
Think carefully.
Not a word.
We must **pretend to fight** to deceive our father, or he'll arrest us both! Draw your sword.

YIELD! GO TO MY FATHER! BRING LIGHT! BRING TORCHES!
Flee, Brother. Farewell!
HELP, FATHER, HELP!
Some **blood** on me will make me look as though I fought fiercely.
Where's the **villain**?
He stood in the dark, sword drawn! I **bleed, sir**! He's fled, when he couldn't –
After him!

What do you mean by "When he couldn't ..."?
When he couldn't persuade me to kill you!
I told him the gods hate children who kill their fathers, and that there was a sacred bond between father and child. Seeing I was opposed to his plan, he wounded me and ran away.
Let him try and run! He'll be caught and executed. Noble Cornwall arrives tonight. I'll use his authority to proclaim that anyone who brings the murderous coward to justice will be rewarded.
And anyone who hides Edgar will suffer death!

When I realised he was **determined** to kill you, I threatened to expose him. He replied ...

... you are **illegitimate** and **worthless**.

No one will believe you over me. I'll deny **everything**, even the letter I wrote. **Everyone** will think you are trying to **frame** me!

Monstrous villain! Did Edgar really say he would deny the letter he wrote?

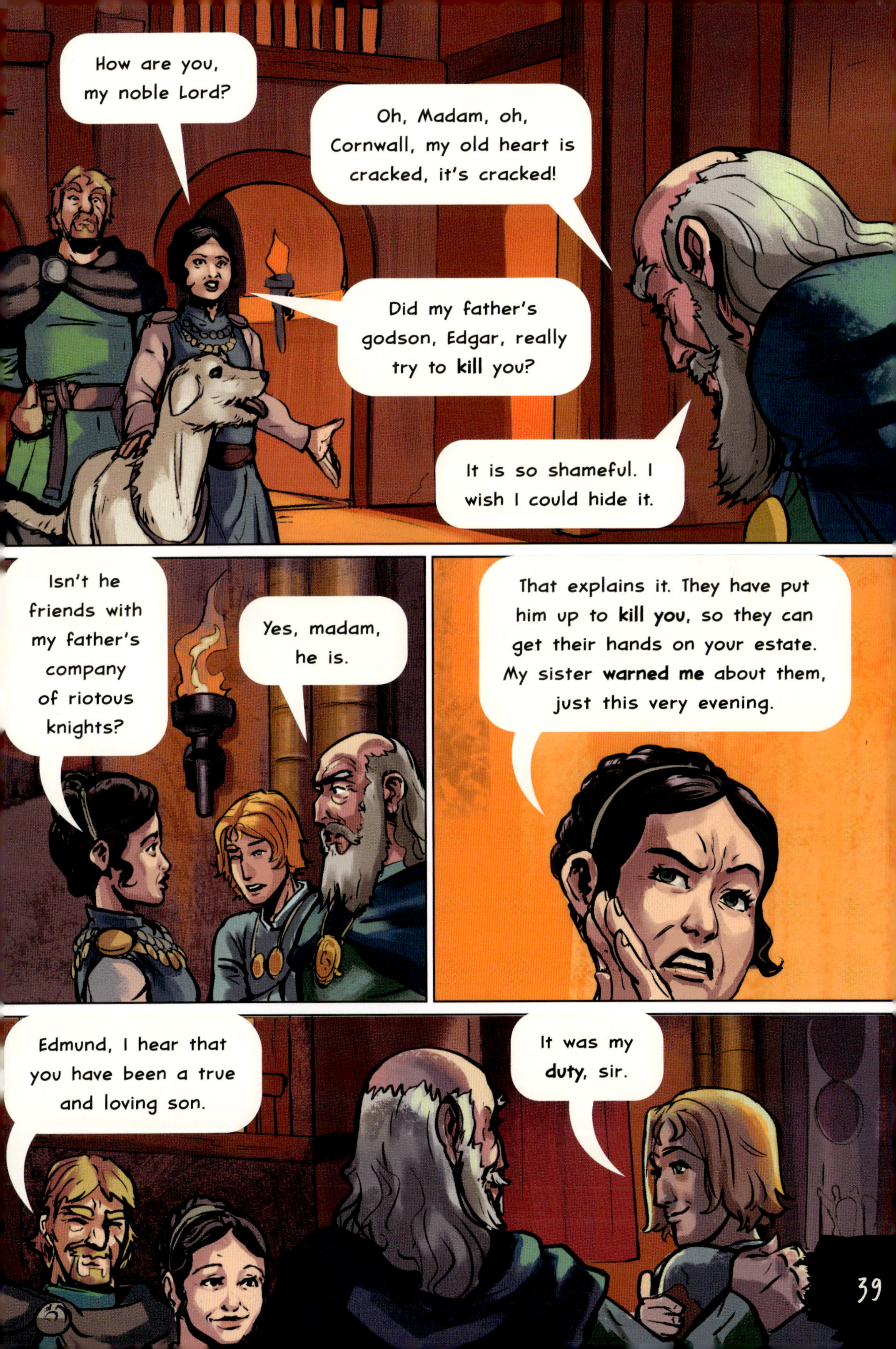

How are you, my noble Lord?
Oh, Madam, oh, Cornwall, my old heart is cracked, it's cracked!
Did my father's godson, Edgar, really try to **kill** you?
It is so shameful. I wish I could hide it.

He **stopped** Edgar's plans and received this wound trying to apprehend him.
Is Edgar being **hunted**?
Ay, my good Lord Cornwall.

If he's caught, we **won't** have to worry about him **ever again**. Edmund, your virtue has been clear throughout. You will serve me. I need trustworthy men like you.
I will serve you **truly** and **faithfully**.

Now, we need your advice. My father and my sister have both written to me about an **argument** they have had.

The messengers from Goneril and the King are outside waiting for my reply. Good friend, we need your advice.

I am at your service, Madam. You are welcome here.

MEANWHILE, AT THE ENTRANCE TO GLOUCESTER'S CASTLE
Where can I stable my horse?
Please tell me, my friend.
In the bog!
I'm **not** your friend.
Why are you acting like this towards me? I don't know you.
Fellow, I know you.
What do you know about me?
You're a **knave** and a **rascal**. You're **filthy** and **arrogant**, **shallow** and **shameless**. And if you deny any of these words, I'll beat you up!
What a **monstrous** fellow you are. You don't know me, and I don't know you!
You **liar**! I tripped you up in front of the King! Draw your sword! I'm going to **stab** you so many times, **moonlight** will shine through your body!

You're here with letters, plotting against the King and taking the side of that puppet, Goneril.
Draw your sword! **Fight!**
HELP! MURDER! HELP!
What is this? **Stop fighting!**
I'll fight you instead, young master!
Stop, or you will **die**! What is this problem between you?
No two opposites could **hate** each other more than me and this scoundrel. I don't like his face.
Perhaps you don't like mine, either ...
I'll be honest, sire, I've seen **better faces**.
What offence did you give him?
None! Never! The King, his master, hit me, and then this fellow tripped me up. Although I didn't fight back, the King **praised** him for this attack. And now he's attacked me **again**!
Bring out the stocks! You **stubborn**, **ancient knave**, we'll teach you!

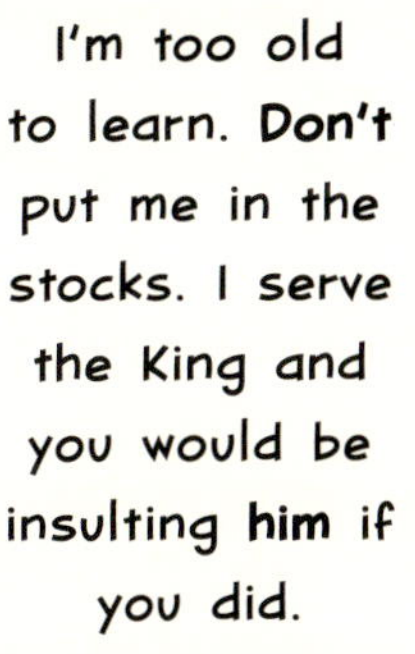

I'm too old to learn. **Don't** put me in the stocks. I serve the King and you would be insulting **him** if you did.
Fetch the stocks! You'll stay there until noon.
Only until noon? **No**, until **night**!

Why, madam, you wouldn't treat me like this if I was your father's **dog**.
No, but you're his **servant**, so I **will**.

I beseech your Grace **not** to do this. The King will **not** be pleased at his messenger being treated like this.
I'll be responsible for it. Put his feet in the stocks.

I am **sorry** for this, friend. I'll try and persuade the Duke to release you.
Don't worry, I've been travelling long and hard. I'll catch up on sleep!
The Duke is to blame. The King **won't be happy** about this.

Ah, well, at least I can now read this letter from Cordelia.

So, Fortune's wheel turns. I was a Duke; now I'm a prisoner. Cordelia was a princess; now she's in exile. Cordelia knows about my disguise and is going to try and put right what is wrong in this country.
I'm exhausted. I'll close my eyes and sleep so I can't see my own **shameful** situation. Good night, Fortune. Turn your wheel and smile upon me once more.
COUNTRYSIDE, NEAR GLOUCESTER'S CASTLE.
I have been proclaimed an **outlaw**. No port or road is safe for me. Luckily, I've escaped my hunters by hiding in this hollow tree.
I'll disguise myself as a lowly beggar and pretend that I am mad.
I've seen Bedlam beggars, who **shriek** and **stab** their own arms with pins and nails. They force poor villagers to give them charity. **"Poor Tom"** they call themselves. At least that's something. As Edgar, I am **nothing**.

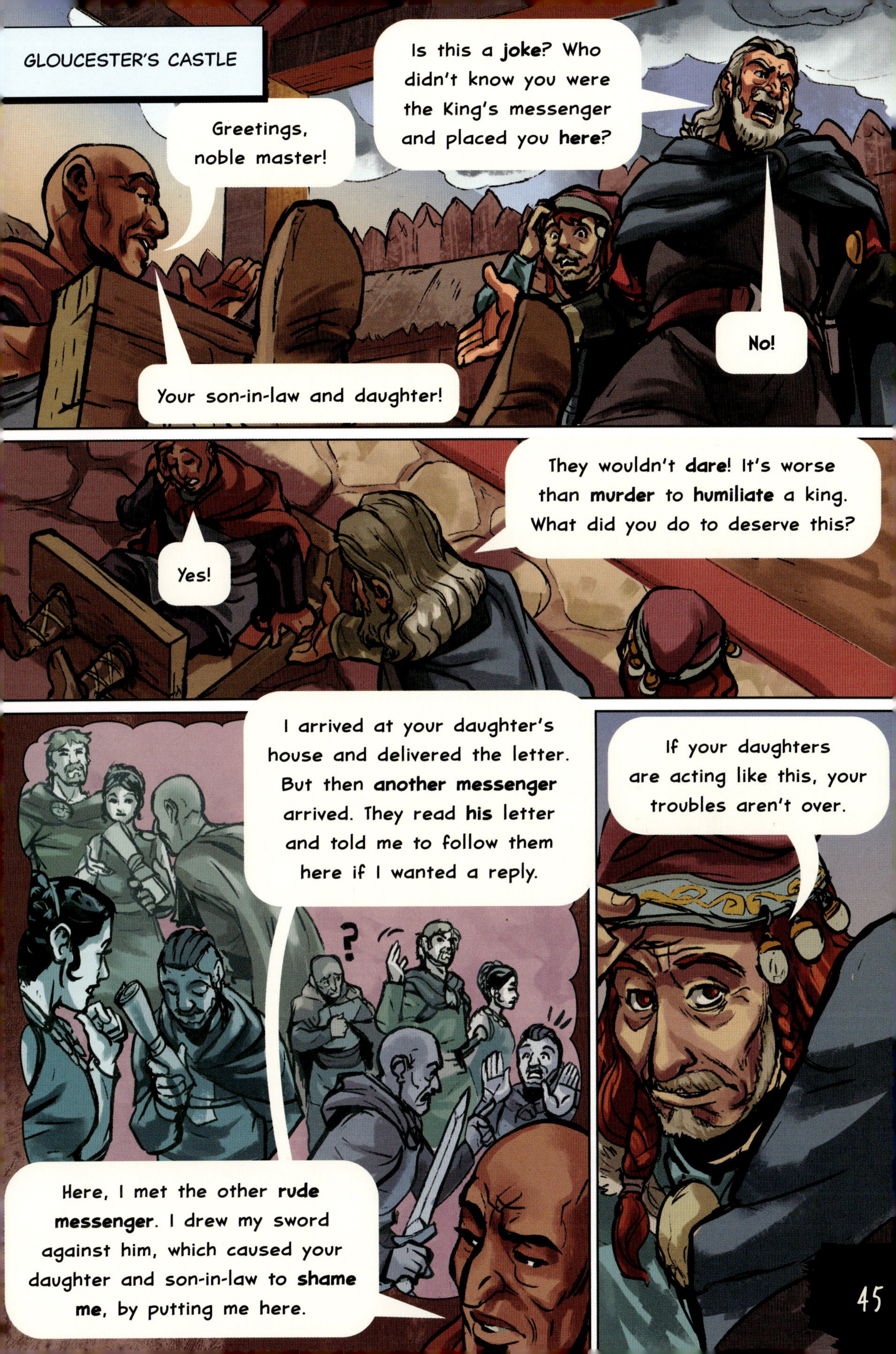

GLOUCESTER'S CASTLE

Greetings, noble master!

Is this a **joke**? Who didn't know you were the King's messenger and placed you **here**?

Your son-in-law and daughter!

No!

Yes!

They wouldn't **dare**! It's worse than **murder** to **humiliate** a king. What did you do to deserve this?

I arrived at your daughter's house and delivered the letter. But then **another messenger** arrived. They read **his** letter and told me to follow them here if I wanted a reply.

Here, I met the other **rude messenger**. I drew my sword against him, which caused your daughter and son-in-law to **shame me**, by putting me here.

I want to speak with the Duke of Cornwall and his wife.
I have informed them, but they will **not** see you.
This is **rebellion**! Have my servant released and tell them I will talk to them **immediately**!
I will. I want there to be peace between you.
Oh, my heart! But I'll **restrain** my rage!
I am glad to see you, your Highness.
I believe you are. Oh, beloved Regan, your sister, Goneril, is **worthless**! She's torn me apart with her **unkindness**.
Please calm down, sir. I'm **sure** she wouldn't neglect her duties to you. If she has **restrained** your riotous knights, then she **must** have a good reason for it.
My **curses** on her!

Sir, you are towards the end of your life. Let yourself be **ruled** by someone who understands you better than you do. Go back to Goneril's house and **apologise**.

Never! She's taken away half of my knights and spoken to me like a serpent! May she get **sick** and **lightning** strike her eyes. May a **poisonous fog** blister her face!
Oh, blessed gods! You'll wish the same on me when your mood is like this!
I'll **never** curse you, blessed Regan. Your tenderness will **never** become harsh. You will **never reduce** my number of knights. You will remember I gave you half of my kingdom and be grateful.

It's my sister arriving. Her letter said she would.

I won't trouble you anymore, Goneril. I'll **never** see you again. *You* are still my flesh and blood or, rather, a **disease** in my flesh. I'm going to stay with **Regan** – with my hundred knights.

Why do you **need** twenty-five, ten or even **five** when you will be in a house with plenty of servants to take care of you?
Why do you even need **one**?

Even **beggars** have things they don't really need! May the heavens give this frail old man a noble anger and **do not** let me cry! You **unnatural hags**, I will have such revenge on you both! But, I will break into a thousand pieces before I weep. Oh, Fool, I shall go **mad**!

Let us go in; there is a great storm coming.
Our house is too small. I will welcome the old man but none of his followers.
Nor I.

The King is in a rage. I don't know where he intends to go. The storm comes. He won't have any shelter.
Then he'll learn his lesson for his **foolishness**.

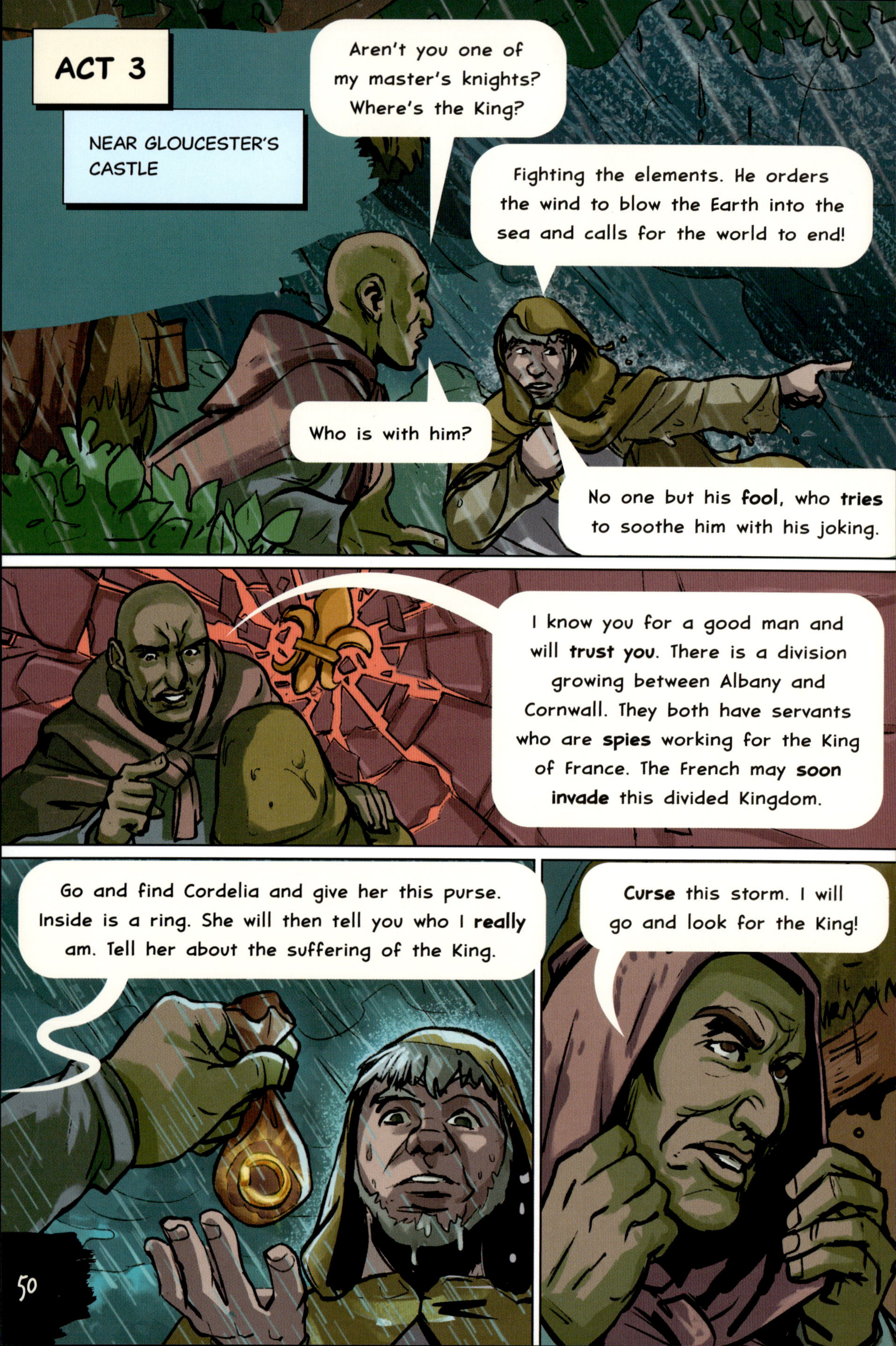

ACT 3

NEAR GLOUCESTER'S CASTLE

Aren't you one of my master's knights? Where's the King?

Fighting the elements. He orders the wind to blow the Earth into the sea and calls for the world to end!

Who is with him?

No one but his **fool**, who **tries** to soothe him with his joking.

I know you for a good man and will **trust you**. There is a division growing between Albany and Cornwall. They both have servants who are **spies** working for the King of France. The French may **soon invade** this divided Kingdom.

Go and find Cordelia and give her this purse. Inside is a ring. She will then tell you who I **really** am. Tell her about the suffering of the King.

ON A HEATH NEAR GLOUCESTER'S CASTLE
Blow, winds, and crack your cheeks! Rage, blow, you cataracts and hurricanoes. Pour out water until you have drowned our steeples! You deadly lightning, singe my white hair And you, thunder, crush the round world flat!
Please, Uncle, let us go inside and ask your daughters to forgive you. This stormy night pities neither wise men nor fools.
Rumble your belly, thunder! Spit, fire! Pour down, rain! Be as horrible as you can. Here I stand your slave – a poor, weak and despised old man.
But I can accuse you of taking my daughters' side, to strike my old, white head! It is foul!

Alas, sir, are you here? Even creatures of the night avoid storms like these.
May the great gods that keep this turmoil above our heads, bring down their fury on those who deserve punishment!
Tremble, those who have committed crimes in **secret**. Hide yourself, you murderers, liars and those who plot against others. I am a man more **sinned against** than **sinning**.
My gracious Lord, there is a hovel nearby. It will give you shelter. Go there and rest, while I again ask for help from your **heartless** daughters.
I begin to see things **differently**. Come on, my boy. Where is this hovel? In times of need, **worthless** things can be **precious**.
He that has a little tiny wit,
With a hey, ho, the wind and the rain,
Must be content with what he gets,
For the rain it raineth, every day.

MEANWHILE, BACK AT GLOUCESTER'S CASTLE
Alas, Edmund. I do not like this unnatural business. When I asked if I could help the King, the Duke and Duchess of Cornwall **took away** the command of my own house!
They **ordered** me never to speak of him again or help **him**, or I would suffer their everlasting displeasure.

How **savage** and **unnatural**!
There is **worse** news. Tonight, I received a letter that is **too dangerous** to discuss, so I've locked it away. The wrongs done to the King will be avenged. Armed forces from France have already landed.

We **must** take the King's side. I will look for him and secretly **help** him. There are **strange things** coming. Be careful, Edmund. Farewell.

I'll tell the Duke all about this, straight away! I'll be **rewarded** for it, and gain everything my father **loses**. The young will **rise** when the old **fall**!

OUTSIDE THE HOVEL ON THE HEATH
Here is the place. Good my Lord, enter.
Let me alone. Will you break my heart?
I would rather break my own. Enter.
This angry, soaking storm is nothing. The storm in my mind, caused by my ungrateful children, takes away all my senses.
To shut me out on a night like this! Oh, Regan, Goneril, your kind old father who gave you everything ...
But no ... That way madness lies. No more of those thoughts.
In, boy. You go first.

The poor, dispossessed wretches with no roof over their heads and hungry stomachs, how can they survive storms such as these? When I was King, I should have done **more** for them.
Those who are **rich** should experience what **wretches feel**. Give them your surplus riches and so make the world a more just and **equal** place.
DEEP WATER! DEEP WATER! POOR TOM!
???
Don't come in, Uncle! There's a ghost in here! He says his name is 'Poor Tom'. **Help me!**
Who are you in there, grumbling in the straw? **Come out!**

Go away! The **devil** follows me!

Did you give **everything** to your **daughters** to become like this?

Who gives **anything** to Poor Tom?

Tom's cold! Oh, do, de, do, de, do, de. Be **kind** to Poor Tom, who is tormented by the devil.

Have his daughters' actions brought him to this?

He has no daughters, sir.

Nothing could cause this, but the actions of unkind daughters!

Pillicock sat on Pillicock's hill.
Alow, alow, loo, loo!
This cold night will turn us all into **fools** and **madmen**.

Is this all a man is? Being naked, you don't owe the silkworm for silk, the cow for leather or the sheep for wool. The three of us are supposedly **sophisticated**, but you, Tom, are the **real** human.

A naked man is nothing but a poor, two-legged animal. **Off with my clothes!**
Stop, Uncle! It's a wicked night for swimming!

Look, here comes a walking fire!
That is the devil, Flibbertigibbet!

Who **are** you? What are your names?
Poor Tom, who eats frogs, toads, tadpoles and wall-newts.
Doesn't your Grace have **better** companions than these?

BACK AT GLOUCESTER'S CASTLE, HIS SON EDMUND IS CONFRONTED BY THE DUKE OF CORNWALL.
I now understand that it wasn't **just** your brother's evil nature that made him want to kill your father. Gloucester's nature **deserved** it!
I will have my **revenge** on your father before I leave this house!
I'm afraid to think how I might be criticised for letting my loyalty to you override my duty to my father.
Here is the letter that my father spoke of. It **proves** he has been spying for France! I **wish** that this treason were not so, and that it was **not me** that detected it!
If the letter is **true**, you have a mighty business to deal with.
True or false, this letter has made you Earl of Gloucester. Seek out where your father is, so we can arrest him.
If I find him helping the King, it will make him look even more guilty!
I will continue to be **loyal** to you, although it **conflicts** with my blood duty to my father.
I will put my trust in **you**. You'll find **me** a **better** father than Gloucester.

INSIDE THE HOVEL
It is better in here than the open air. I'll try and make it more comfortable for you. I won't be gone long.
Lear's **rage** is driving him **mad**! May the gods reward your kindness.
A dancing devil calls out to me! Beware the foul fiend!
May a **thousand devils** with burning forks **strike** my daughters!
Oh, pity! Where is this self control, you used to boast that you had, My Lord?
I feel **so sorry** for him, that I could cry and give away my disguise.
Even the little **dogs** bark at me!

Begone, you mongrels! Tom will make you weep and wail. And with my howling, they are all gone!

Come, my Lord. Lie here and rest awhile.
Make no noise; make no noise. We'll go to supper in the morning.

And I'll go to bed at noon.

Where is the King?
Here, sir, but do not trouble him. His mind has gone.
Pick him up. There is a **plot to kill him**! Outside there is a carriage. Put him in it and drive to Dover, where you will find protection.

If you delay, he, and those who help him, will **surely die**.
Come away immediately!

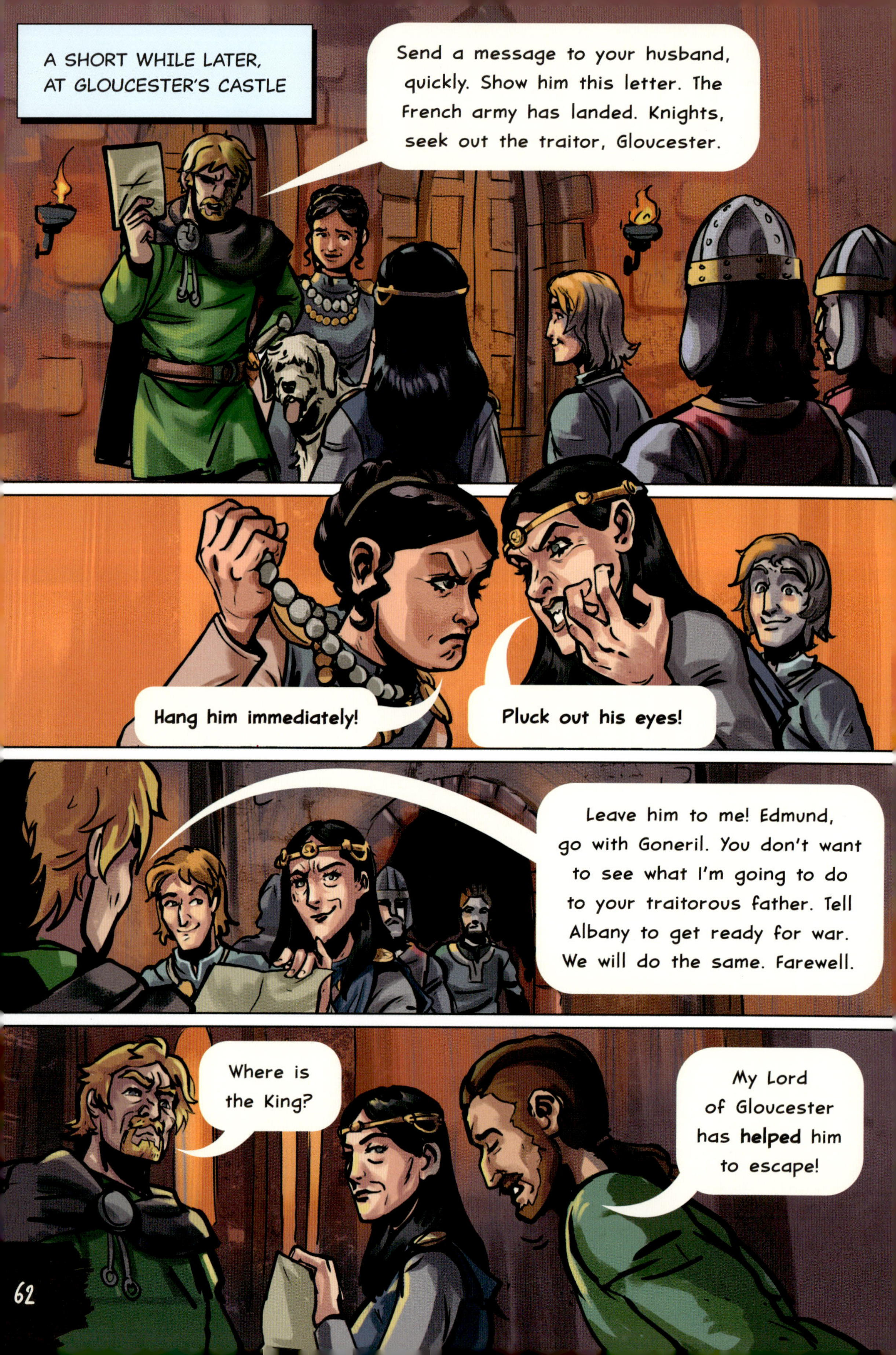

A SHORT WHILE LATER, AT GLOUCESTER'S CASTLE

Send a message to your husband, quickly. Show him this letter. The French army has landed. Knights, seek out the traitor, Gloucester.

Hang him immediately!

Pluck out his eyes!

Thirty-six of Lear's knights, and some of Gloucester's servants, have gone with him towards Dover. They say they have well-armed friends there.
Prepare the horses for your mistress.

Farewell, sweet Lord and sister.
Edmund, farewell.

Go and seek the traitor, Gloucester. Tie his arms and bring him here.

I cannot condemn him to death **without** trial, but I can use my power to show how angry I am!

The ungrateful fox, Gloucester!
Bind fast his withered arms! **Tie him to the chair!**

Good friends, you are **my guests**. Don't treat me like this!
Bind him!
Tighter! You **filthy traitor!**
Unmerciful lady, I am **no** traitor! What are you doing?
What letters have you received from France?
And **don't** lie! We know the truth.
The traitors to whom you've sent the **lunatic King!**
Where have you sent the King?
To Dover.
Why to Dover? Weren't you ordered to have **no** dealings with him? Why to Dover?

Why to Dover? I'll tell you.
Because I would not see your cruel nails **pluck out** his poor old eyes, or your fierce sister's fangs **rip** into his flesh. You sent him out into the storm and had no pity. I will see **vengeance** on you, you cruel children.

You won't see anything **ever again**! Hold the chair. Upon your eyes, I'll set my foot!

Help me! Oh, you gods!

ARGHHHHHH!

Now his face looks uneven! Pull out the **other** eye too.

Stop, my Lord!
Don't do this thing!
How dare you?!
You **villain**!
How now,
you **dog**?!
Come on, then.
Fight me!
How **dare**
you defy us?!
I am **slain**! My
Lord, you have
one eye left to
see that Cornwall
comes to harm.

Then I'll stop him from seeing more. Out, vile jelly!
ARGHHHHHH!
Where is your light **now**?
All is dark and comfortless. Where is my son Edmund? He will take revenge on you!
Edmund hates you! He's the one who told us of your treachery. He'll show you **no pity**.
How **stupid** I have been! Edgar was **falsely** accused by the traitor, Edmund. Forgive me, kind gods, and let Edgar prosper!
Throw him out of the gates and let him **smell** his way to Dover!
This wound is more serious than I first thought. Give me your arm.

ACT 4
THE HEATH NEAR GLOUCESTER'S CASTLE, SOMETIME LATER
I am the lowest of the low, but things can only get better for me.
But who comes here? My father with bleeding eyes? **Oh, this world is cruel!**
Get away, good friend. Be gone. Your help can do me no good and may bring you to harm.
But you cannot see your way.
I have **nowhere** to go so I don't need eyes! Oh, my dear, abused, son Edgar. If I could touch your face again, I would not want my eyes back.
I thought I was at my **lowest** and now **this**! Things can always get worse!
It's poor, mad Tom. Where are you going, fellow?
Is it a beggar?
He's a madman **and** a beggar.
I saw a man like that in last night's storm.

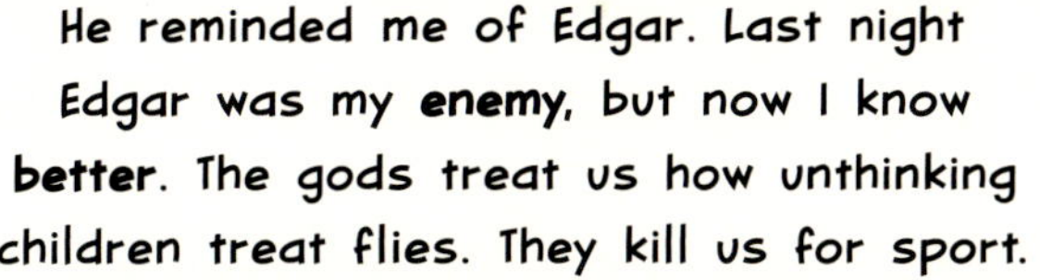
He reminded me of Edgar. Last night Edgar was my **enemy**, but now I know **better**. The gods treat us how unthinking children treat flies. They kill us for sport.

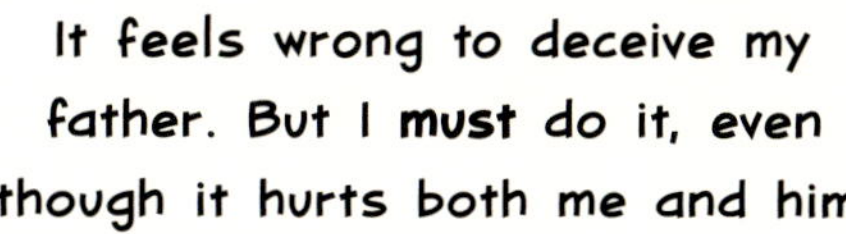
It feels wrong to deceive my father. But I **must** do it, even though it hurts both me and him.

Bless thee, master.

Is that the naked fellow?
Ay, my Lord.
Then you can go. If you still want to help me, catch up with us on the road to Dover and bring some clothes for this poor being. I will ask him to lead me on.
But he is **mad**!
It is the curse of our times that the mad must lead the blind. Do as I bid.

Naked fellow! Come here!
I **cannot** keep up this act anymore, but I **must**!

Bless your sweet eyes. They bleed.

Do you know the way to Dover?

I know every inch of the way.

THE CASTLE OF ALBANY AND GONERIL

Where is my husband and your master?

Inside, but he is acting **very** strangely.

I told him you were arriving, and he said, "Curse her."

I told him of Gloucester's treachery and Edmund's loyal service, and he called me "a fool", and said I had got it all wrong.

Come no further, Edmund. My husband is too much of a **coward** to join our side. Our feelings towards each other may soon be fulfilled.

Go help Cornwall gather his army. I must take over the duties of my **husband** and make **him** play the **wife**! We can send messages to each other by this servant. And, **if you dare,** we will soon be lovers.

Bend to me...

If that kiss could **speak**, it would make you do **great** things. Understand this and so, farewell.
I'm your servant until I die...
Dearest Edmund!
Oh, the difference between **him** and my **foolish husband**!
Madam, your husband.
So, you've finally **bothered** to come and see me!
Oh, Goneril, you are **not** worth the **dust** that the rude wind blows in your face.
You **cowardly man**! You **always** turn the other cheek, letting others insult you and take advantage of your weak nature.
You're a fine one to talk! You behave more like a **devil** than a **wife**!

On one hand, I am **glad** that Cornwall is **dead**, but on the other, Regan is now a widow. And she will be with **my** Edmund soon! He might choose her! That would force me to continue my **hateful life** with Albany!

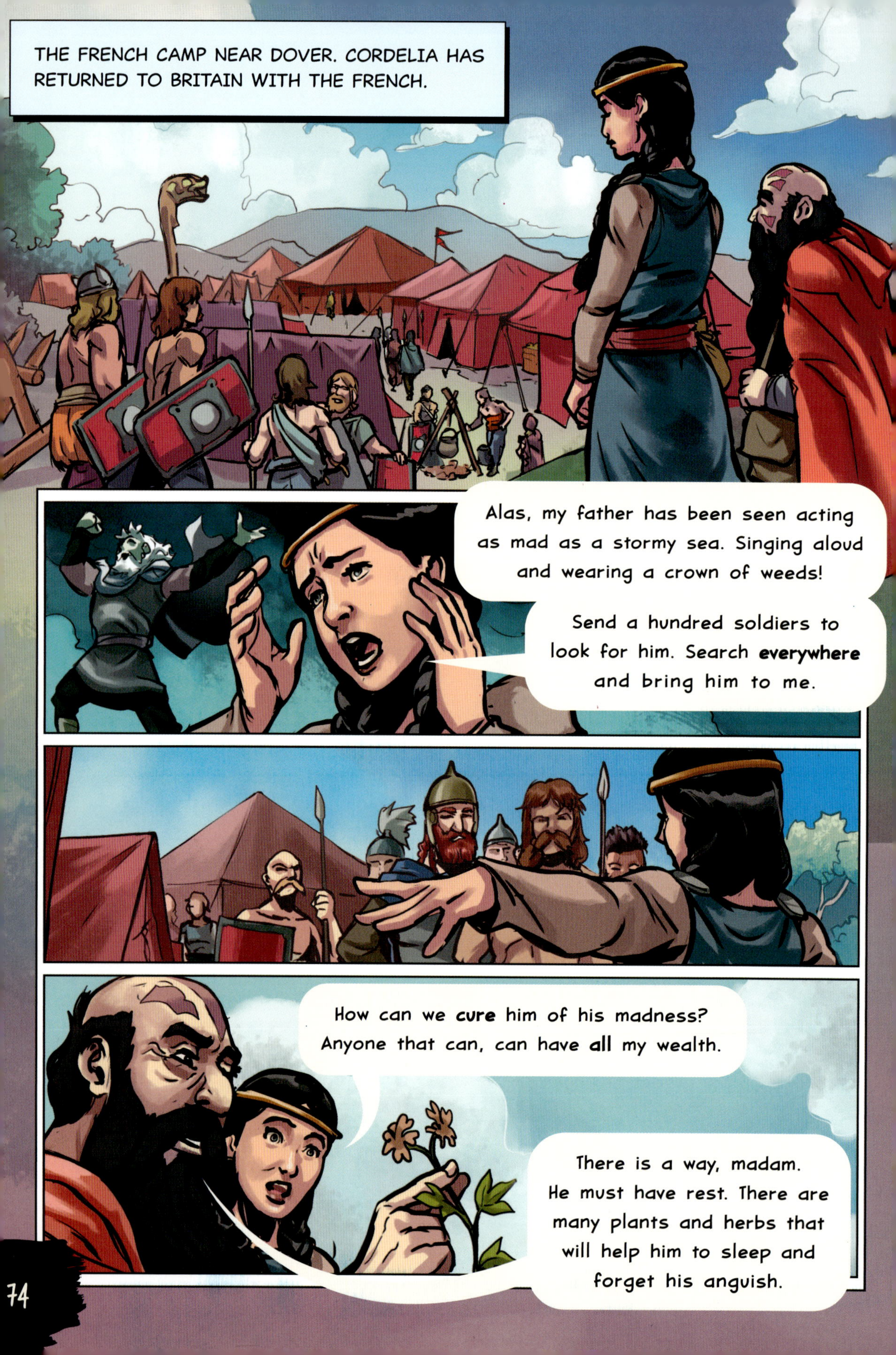

THE FRENCH CAMP NEAR DOVER. CORDELIA HAS RETURNED TO BRITAIN WITH THE FRENCH.

Alas, my father has been seen acting as mad as a stormy sea. Singing aloud and wearing a crown of weeds!

Send a hundred soldiers to look for him. Search **everywhere** and bring him to me.

All you secret, healing plants of the Earth, my tears will help you grow. May you heal the **good man's** distress.
Go and find those plants, before his uncontrollable rage takes away his life.
News, madam. The British forces are marching towards us.
We knew this and are **ready** for them.
Dear Father, I am doing this all for **you**. My husband, the King of France, listened to my tearful pleading and **invaded** this country.
We are not fighting for pure ambition, but for **love**, dear love, and our aged father's **rights**. Hopefully, I may soon hear and see him.

MEANWHILE, AT GLOUCESTER'S CASTLE
Are Albany's forces on the move?
Ay, madam.
Is he there in person?
Ay, madam. But he makes a fuss about nothing. Your sister Goneril is a **better soldier**!
Did Lord Edmund speak to your master?
No, madam.
What was in my sister's letter to him?
I don't know, Lady.
It was **foolish** to let Gloucester live, once we had put out his eyes. **Everyone** now **hates** us!
I think Edmund has gone to **end** his father's sorry life, and to find out the strength of the French army.
I must go after Gloucester with this letter, madam.
Our troops leave tomorrow. Stay with us. The roads are dangerous.
I **cannot**, madam. My lady told me to go.

Why would she write to Edmund? Can't you just speak the message to him? I would love you greatly if you let me read my sister's letter.
Open it.
Madam, I'd rather not ...

I know your lady does not love her husband, Albany. When she was here, she and Edmund exchanged many strange and loving looks. I know you are in her confidence.
Me, Madam?!

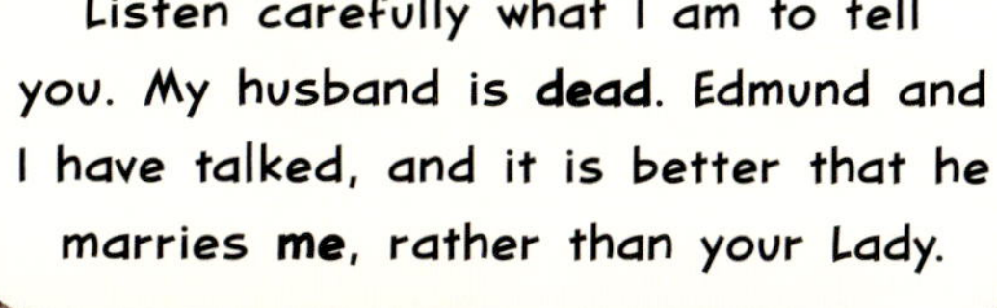
Listen carefully what I am to tell you. My husband is dead. Edmund and I have talked, and it is better that he marries me, rather than your Lady.

If you find Edmund, give him this. And when you talk to your lady of this, make her come to her senses and see reason. And if you come across the blind traitor Gloucester, well, there will be promotion for anyone that kills him ...

Farewell.
If I meet Gloucester, I will show whose side I am on.

NEAR DOVER, NEXT MORNING.

When will we come to the top of the cliff?

We are climbing it now. It is a **hard** climb.

I think the ground is flat and even.

No, it's **horribly steep**. Can you hear the sea?

No, truly.

Then the damage done to your eyes is affecting your **other** senses.

It may be so. I think your voice is different – you speak better than you did before.

You are deceived. Only my clothes are changed.

We're here! How fearful it is to look down from such a height. The flying birds are as small as beetles. The fishermen on the beach look like mice. I'll look no more in case my head spins and I topple down head-first.

Put me where you are standing.

You are now within a **foot** of the edge. I wouldn't jump for all the riches in the world.

If this doesn't shock him out of his despair, nothing will!

Leave me, sir. Farewell.

Who are you, sir?

Did I fall?

Yes! I was walking along the beach, when I saw you plummet down the chalky cliff. I hurried over and found you still alive! It is a **miracle**! See how **high** the cliff is!

I have no eyes.

I recognise that voice. Is it the **King**?

Ay, every inch a king!

Oh, let me kiss your hand!

Let me clean it first. It smells of **death**.

Oh, ruined piece of nature! Do you know me?

I remember your eyes! Do you squint at me?

I can see nothing.

A man without eyes can still see how the world works. Get yourself glass eyes and, like a scheming politician, pretend to see things that **aren't** there. If you want to cry about my ill fortune, then take my eyes.

He speaks both **sense** and **nonsense** together!

THE DOCTOR ARRIVES ...

Hail, gentle sir. Have you heard of a battle nearby?
Everyone has. The enemy draws near. The Queen of France is here but her forces have moved on.
Thank you, sir.
I will never again think of killing myself. Now, good sir, who are you?
A most poor man, who has suffered fortune's blows, and, because of this, has now learnt to pity others. Give me your hand. I'll lead you somewhere to rest.
Hearty thanks. May Heaven reward you.
There is the traitor Gloucester! Prepare yourself for death! You! Peasant! Get away from this traitor!
Keep away, I'm warning you ...
Let go or you die!

You have killed me! Take this letter to Edmund, Duke of Gloucester, and he will reward you. He is with the English army.
Let us see what this letter **says**.
It's from Goneril to Edmund. They are plotting to **kill her husband**, the King's friend, Albany, so they can be married! I will show this wicked letter to the Duke when the time is right!
I think I can hear the distant drums. Come, give me your hand. I will take you to a friend.

THE FRENCH CAMP NEAR DOVER
Thank you, Kent, I can never repay you for your goodness.
To be thanked by you is enough.
You should change those clothes for something that suits you better.
Sorry madam, but I do not wish to reveal who I really am until the time is right. And I beg that you pretend not to know me.
How is the King?
He sleeps.
Oh, kind gods, cure the great wound in his mind, caused by his children.
Oh my dear father, may these lips **heal** you, and let this kiss **repair** all the **violent harms** that my sisters have done to you. It's a wonder you didn't die. He's waking ...
How are you, my royal Lord?
Where have I been? Where am I? Is it daytime? I have been mightily abused! I do not know what to say!

Look upon me and give me your blessing!
Do not **mock** me! I am a **foolish** old man. I fear I am not in my right mind. I should know you and this man here.

Do not laugh at me, but I **think** this lady here is my daughter, Cordelia.
And so I am, **so I am!**

Pray, do not weep. If you have **poison** for me, then I will **drink** it. I know you **do not** love me. Your sisters have, I know, done me wrong. You have good reason to **hate** me, they do not.
No reason, no reason.
Am I in France?

No, in your own kingdom, sir.
His rage is over, but do not trouble him until he is settled.
Do not deceive me.
You must bear with me. Please forget and forgive. I am **old and foolish**.
Will it please your highness to walk?

ACT 5

THE BRITISH CAMP NEAR DOVER

Something has happened to Oswald, my sister's messenger.

I fear you are right.

Now, my sweet Lord, I know I have promised to **marry** you, but don't you love my sister, Goneril?

Only with **honourable** love.

I will **not** have her as a **rival**. Do not be **intimate** with her.

I won't. I **promise**, by my **honour**.

Here she comes with her husband, Albany! Let us greet them.

The King has joined with his daughter, Cordelia, along with other rebels who are complaining about the harshness of our rule.

We must **unite** against the enemy and **put aside** any personal differences.

We will gather a council of war to plan our attack.

I will meet you at your tent.

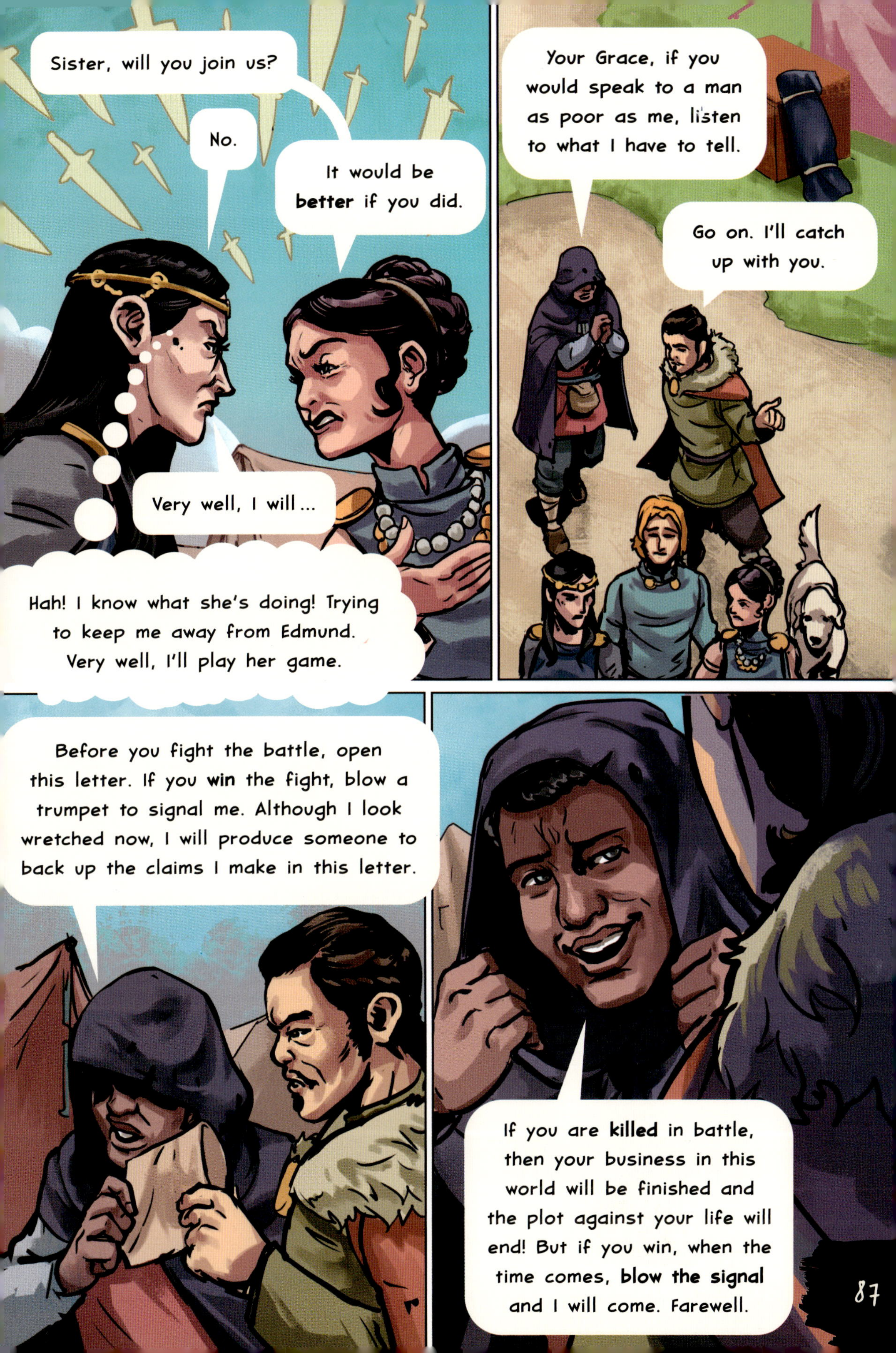

Sister, will you join us?

No.

It would be **better** if you did.

Very well, I will ...

Hah! I know what she's doing! Trying to keep me away from Edmund. Very well, I'll play her game.

Your Grace, if you would speak to a man as poor as me, listen to what I have to tell.

Go on. I'll catch up with you.

I'll use Albany's power to **win** the battle. Then when it's over, Goneril can work out how to **kill** him. Albany intends to show mercy to Lear and Cordelia after the battle. But if I take them prisoner, they will **never** get that pardon. **They will be dead!**

My plans need actions, not words!

THE COUNTRYSIDE NEAR DOVER

The battle is about to begin! Stay here. Pray that **goodness** will win the day. If I ever return to you again, I will bring good news.

God go with you, sir.

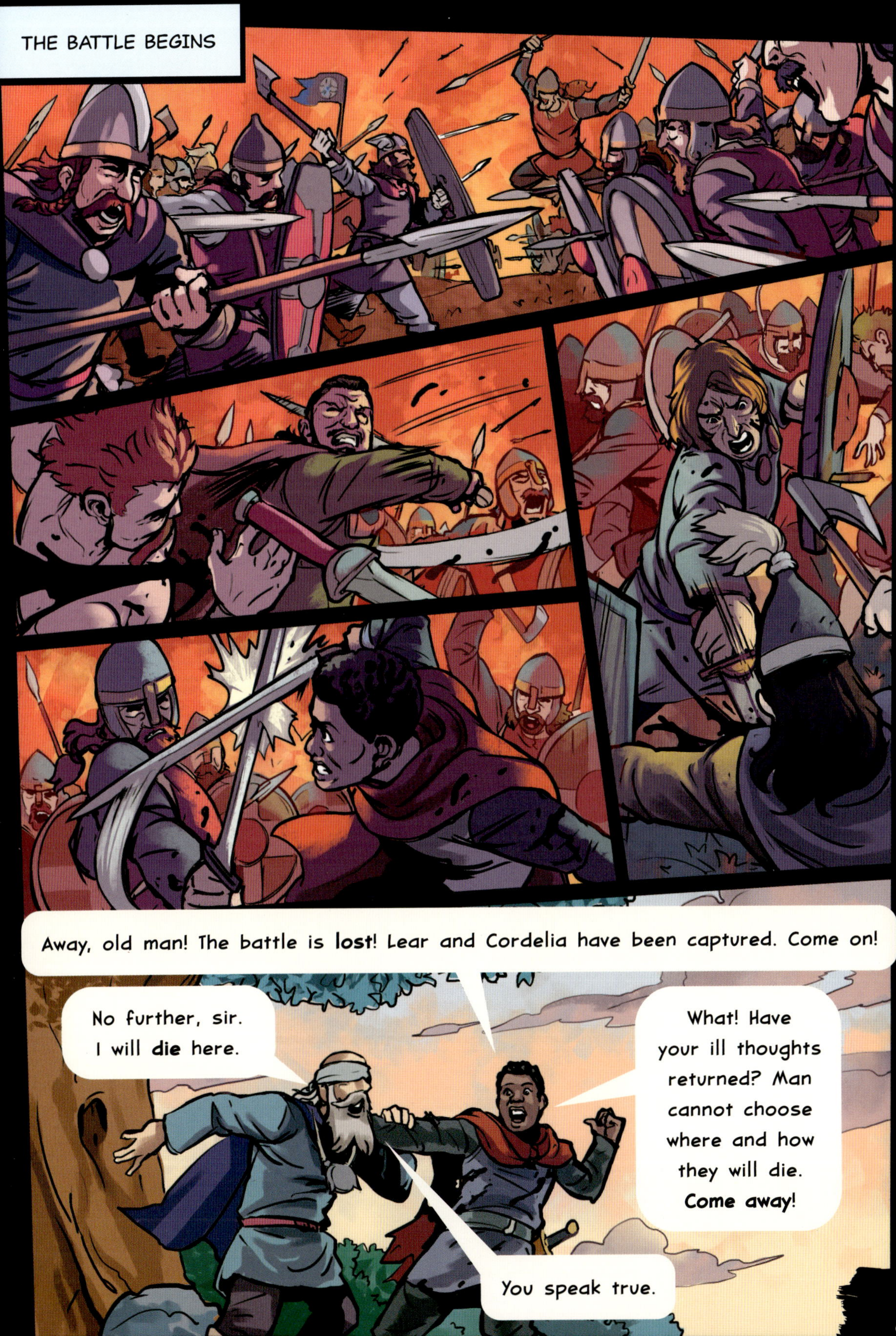

THE BATTLE BEGINS

THE BRITISH CAMP NEAR DOVER
Take them away! Guard them well until we decide what to do with them.
We are not the first whose good intentions have made everything **worse**! I'm sad for you, dear King. Shall we speak to my sisters, your daughters?
No, no, no! Let's go to prison. We'll live, pray and sing and be happy together. We will never be separated. Wipe away your tears. Come.
Captain, follow them to prison and carry out the instructions in this letter. If you do so, you will be **richly rewarded**. Say you'll do it, or I'll find someone else.
I'll do it.
Sir, you have shown **true courage** today and captured the enemy leaders. I now need to take them and treat them with the honour that is due to them, and what is best for the country.

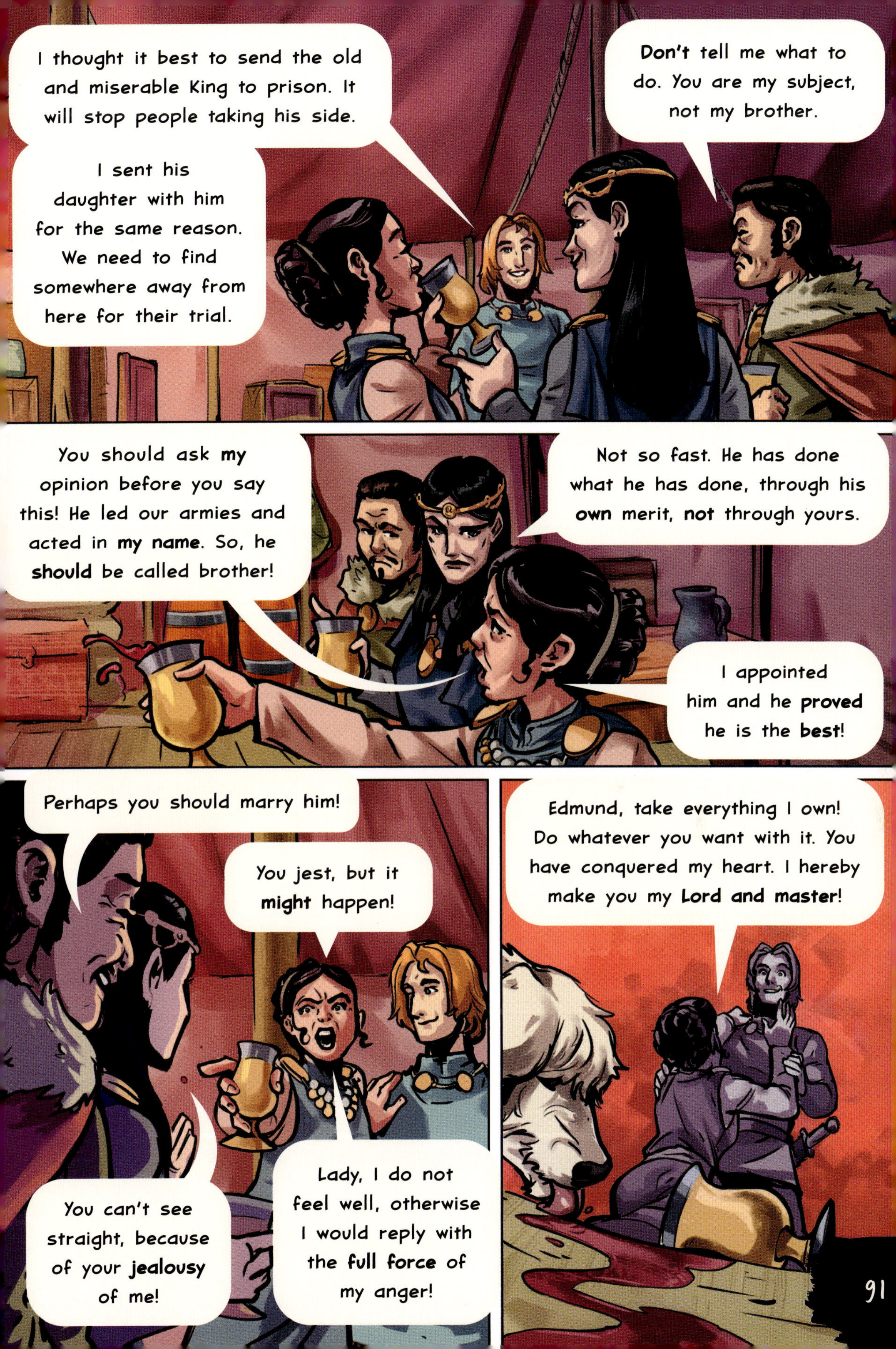

I thought it best to send the old and miserable King to prison. It will stop people taking his side.

I sent his daughter with him for the same reason. We need to find somewhere away from here for their trial.

Don't tell me what to do. You are my subject, not my brother.

You should ask **my** opinion before you say this! He led our armies and acted in **my name**. So, he **should** be called brother!

Not so fast. He has done what he has done, through his **own** merit, **not** through yours.

I appointed him and he **proved** he is the **best**!

You have no right to grant such a gift.
You have no right to deny it, Lord.
The purity of my blood gives me that right.
Your illegitimate birth means you can never accept what this woman offers.
Edmund, fight anyone who says you can't be mine!

Edmund, I arrest you for high treason! This snake, Goneril, is your accomplice. She is my wife; if you want to marry her, you'll have to ask my permission! I arrest her, too!

You are armed. Let a trumpet sound and if no one appears to challenge your treachery, then I will fight you myself!
I accept your challenge! Whoever calls me a traitor is a villainous liar! I will fight and prove my honour!

I am sick.
The poison is working!
Take her to my tent. Let the trumpet sound!

If any honourable man wishes to accuse Edmund, Earl of Gloucester, of being a traitor let him appear by the third sound of the trumpet!

Who are you? Why do you take up this challenge?
My name is lost, destroyed by a **treacherous** worm. I come to fight Edmund.

You have betrayed the **gods**, your **brother** and your **father** and now plot against Albany. You are a **filthy, poisonous traitor**!
I don't know you, but I throw these words **back** at you! My sword will write "traitor" on your heart!

You **didn't** have to fight! You have been tricked!
Be quiet, woman, or I'll **close** your mouth with this paper! Read your own evil, and you, lady, also **know** what he has done!

I make the laws, **not you**! You **can't** prosecute me.

I disguised myself and nursed him through his misfortune. I revealed my true identity to him, just half an hour ago, and told him my story. The news was **too much** for him; his **heart broke** and gave out. But he died happy.

Brother, your words make me begin to regret my wickedness.

I was engaged to **both** of them. Now all three of us are united in death.
We do not pity their deaths.
Here is Kent.

There is no time to give you the greeting that you deserve.
I have come to bid my king and master a good night. Is he not here?
How could we have forgotten him?
Speak, Edmund. Where are the King and Cordelia?

I'm dying. I want to do some good. Go to the prison. I have ordered the **execution** of Lear and Cordelia. Tell the captain to stop. **Hurry!**

Run! Run! Oh, run!

Your wife and I gave the order to **hang** Cordelia in the prison and make it look as though she **killed** herself.
The gods defend her. Take this man away.

Howl, howl, howl, howl! Oh, you are men of stones! If I had your tongues to cry out and eyes to weep, I'd use them to crack open Heaven's vault! She's gone forever. She's dead as earth.
Bring me a mirror. If her breath makes a mark on it, she's still alive.
Is this the end of the world?
Oh, my good master!
Please go away.
It is noble Kent, your friend.
A **plague** on you! You are **all** murderers and traitors! I might have saved her, but now she's gone **forever**.
Who are you? My eyes are not the best. Are you not Kent?
The same, my Lord. I **was also** your servant Caius, who came to you when you divided your kingdom and lost your mind.

He is gone.

It is a wonder that he has endured so long.

Bear them away. Our business is now to grieve them.

My two friends, you should now rule this country and heal this damaged nation.

I cannot. For I soon have a journey, sir, to follow my master to the next world.

The next generation, must bear the weight of this. The oldest have suffered the most. We that are young shall never see so much, nor live so long.

THE END

Storytelling in *King Lear*

Other than being set in a pagan Britain (before Christianity arrived), no one truly knows in which period Shakespeare intended to set *King Lear*. Palaces, castles and countryside are mentioned but, other than Dover, no city or town in Britain is named.

The passage of time is also not clear in the play. Lear's descent into madness may come across as unrealistically rapid. Similarly, the time between Cordelia leaving Britain and returning with the French army, is in stark contrast to the back-and-forth domestic squabbles happening between the other two daughters. It is possible that Shakespeare was aware of this and blurred the passage of time for dramatic purposes.

ACT 1 A long first act sets up the plot and sub-plot. *King Lear* sets a "love test" for his daughters. Cordelia, his youngest, refuses to indulge, while her sisters fawn. Lear disowns Cordelia for her honesty. Lear's loyal servant, the Duke of Kent, objects to Cordelia's treatment and is banished. Cordelia marries the King of France and leaves Britain.

In a sub-plot, Edmund, the illegitimate son of Gloucester, tricks his father into believing that Gloucester's legitimate son, Edgar, wishes to kill him and take his title.

Kent returns, disguised, and takes on a role as Lear's servant. Meanwhile, Lear argues with Goneril over the number of knights he is allowed. Lear's Fool jokes about Lear's self-harming behaviour. Lear begins to worry that he is going mad.

ACT 2 This act highlights the themes of deception, cruelty and the disintegration of order in both personal and political terms. Edmund convinces Gloucester of Edgar's treachery. Edgar escapes by disguising himself as "mad" beggar, Poor Tom. Regan and her husband, Cornwall, arrive at Gloucester's house and make friends with Edmund. When Lear arrives, he is confronted by Regan and Goneril, and driven from the house into a terrible storm.

ACT 3 One of Shakespeare's most brutal Acts. The storm on the heath mirrors Lear's rage and descent into madness. Meeting Edgar, disguised as Poor Tom, Lear, Kent and the Fool take refuge in a hovel. Gloucester tracks them down and arranges transport to Dover to meet up with Cordelia and the invading French army. Gloucester is punished by Regan and Cornwall by having his eyes gouged out. A servant tries to stop them, but Regan kills him, though the servant fatally wounds Cornwall.

ACT 4 As the play moves towards its terrible ending, this act explores the themes of betrayal and redemption. Edgar meets his blinded father and leads him to Dover, where Gloucester wishes to kill himself. Edgar tricks Gloucester into believing he has jumped off a cliff but survived. Albany realises that his wife, Goneril, is evil. Goneril wishes to kill Albany and marry Edmund. Edgar kills Oswald, Goneril's steward, and discovers letters between the two sisters that reveal their treacherous plans. Lear is reunited with Cordelia and begins to come back to his senses. However, the battle between English and French armies threatens this happiness.

ACT 5. Death, revelations and reconciliation fill this act, as the drama works its way to its tragic end. The French army, led by Cordelia, is defeated. Lear and Cordelia are taken prisoner by Edmund. Albany accuses Edmund and Goneril of high treason. Edgar, disguised as a knight, challenges Edmund to a duel and fatally wounds him. Goneril poisons Regan and then takes her own life. Before he dies, Edmund reveals (too late) that he has ordered the deaths of Cordelia and Lear. Lear carries in Cordelia's body and then dies himself. Edgar takes the crown to become the new King of Britain, a land once again united.

Sources in *King Lear*

Writers often adapt ideas or themes from other writers and create their own stories. Shakespeare certainly did this. He took stories from earlier times and other languages and adapted them for his audience.

One early example here would be Geoffrey of Monmouth's book from around 1136, *The History of the Kings of Britain,* where he wrote about the legendary King Leir and his daughters. Shakespeare would certainly have read this before embarking on writing his version of Lear's story.

He also drew upon sources closer to his own time. *The True Chronicle Historie of King Leir and his Three Daughters* was an old play that had been performed in London theatres in the early 1590s. This play was very different to Shakespeare's version. There is no Gloucester sub-plot, no Fool, and Cordelia and Lear do not die.

In fact, a few other versions – *The Mirrour for Magistrates* (1574), *Holinshed's Chronicles of England, Scotland and Ireland* (1577) and Book 2 Canto 10 of Edmund Spenser's *Fairie Queene* (1590) – all end "happily-ever-after". Lear is reunited with Cordelia and restored to his throne.

Shakespeare's Gloucester sub-plot may also echo Sir Philip Sydney's, *The Countess of Pembroke's Arcadia* (1590). Part of this recounts the story of a blind king with two sons, one of whom plots against him. When the king finds out about the plotting, he reacts by stating that he wishes to kill himself by throwing himself from a cliff.

Shakespeare also used Samuel Harsnett's *A Declaration of Egregious Popish Imposters* (1603), which criticises fake exorcisms done by priests, as a source for Edgar's words when he's pretending to be possessed by devils.

There were also two "real-life" stories that Shakespeare was surely aware of. At the end of the 1500s, a former mayor of London, Sir William Allen, divided his property among his three daughters. Having obtained their father's property, the daughters turned their backs on him. And in 1603, the eldest daughter of Sir Brian Annesley, along with her husband, tried to get Sir Brian certified as a lunatic in order to control his estate. Sir Brian's youngest daughter (named Cordell!) challenged this decision in court and stopped it.

Themes of *King Lear*

In such a complex play as *King Lear*, there are many themes explored in the course of the action. These are some of the major ones.

"Madness"

Although we would not perhaps use the term "mad" or "madness" nowadays to describe a psychological illness, in Elizabethan and Jacobean times, madness was a common term and could also be used to describe possession by evil spirits and demons. In *King Lear*, madness is portrayed in several ways and has a significant impact on the plot.

Lear's descent into madness is triggered by his own actions. In dividing his kingdom, he gradually loses his power and sanity.

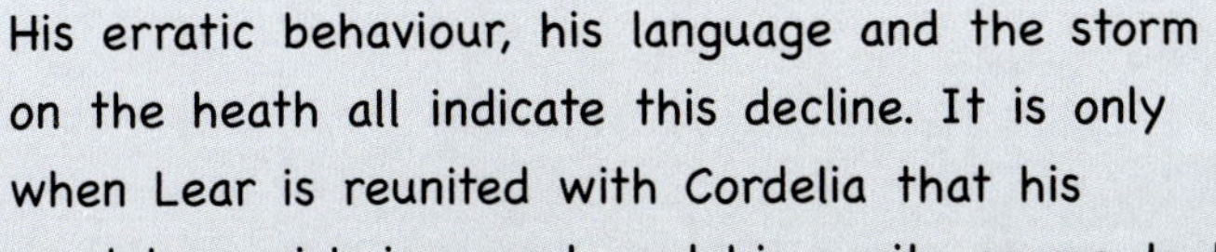

His erratic behaviour, his language and the storm on the heath all indicate this decline. It is only when Lear is reunited with Cordelia that his mental anguish is eased, and his sanity seems to be restored.

The "madness" of people's actions and the situations they create, are critiqued by several characters, especially Lear's Fool. He uses wit and humour to make observations on the folly and madness of the others.

Feigned insanity is also present in *King Lear*, when Edgar pretends to be Poor Tom. Shakespeare had previously explored this idea in his great tragedy, *Hamlet*. Although this is a plot device to allow Edgar to escape capture, the spectacle of a mad beggar was also probably meant to amuse some of the audience who may have visited Bethlehem Hospital (Bedlam) in London to view the inmates, a form of grotesque voyeurism (in this case, the enjoyment of observing others' distress).

Shakespeare uses these different types of mental instability as a way to highlight the vulnerability of human nature and to expose the "madness" of social behaviour and political power.

Family Relationships

The play explores various aspects of family: love, betrayal, loyalty, power and the social and political consequences of family breakup.

These splits begin almost immediately with Lear's love-test. By the end of Act 1, Lear's family has been broken up irrevocably, and Gloucester is embroiled in Edmund's evil plot against his half-brother. The turmoil and chaos that ensue affect the state of the nation and world order.

Only when Lear and Cordelia meet at Dover is there a hope that both justice and order will be restored (although this hope is brutally destroyed with their deaths).

Sibling rivalry is also central to the play. Goneril and Regan's treacherous natures contrast with Cordelia's honesty and loyalty, and their competition for Edmund's affections leads to murder and suicide.

The illegitimate Edmund schemes to replace his legitimate half-brother, Edgar, and take over his father's title and lands. This too leads to tragic and terrible outcomes of mutilation and death.

A glaring absence in the play is the lack of a mother figure. Mothers are not mentioned, other than in Gloucester's explanation of how Edmund was conceived outside of marriage. Perhaps Shakespeare left this gap in honour of the recently deceased Elizabeth I, who, although she never gave birth, was considered to be the mother of the nation.

Nature

The play explores the theme of nature in several ways, including the natural order of power, what is natural and unnatural, and the relationship between humans and the natural world. The words "natural" and "nature" are amongst the most used words in the play.

The natural order of political power is immediately broken by Lear with his decision to divide his kingdom. Lear's self delusion leads him to believe that he is acting naturally, and anyone who goes against his will is "unnatural". It is only through his suffering that he begins to change his view of the natural order.

Natural and unnatural acts are also explored. The barbarism of Cornwall and Regan in blinding Gloucester is an unnatural act, demonstrating cruelty and inhumanity to a fellow human being. In direct contrast to this "unnatural" behaviour, Cordelia's honesty and truth are seen as being "natural" virtues.

To emphasise the inhumanity of both Regan and Goneril, Shakespeare uses animal imagery to highlight their nature. They are likened to animals, such as tigers, vultures, snakes, wolves and dogs, and their animal instincts ultimately lead to their deaths.

Edmund's illegitimate birth is also considered "unnatural", and acts as a spur to plot against his father and more "natural" brother, Edgar.

Shakespeare's Language

Poetry

Shakespeare's works were often written in a mixture of verse and prose (normal speech). Important and high-ranking characters (kings, lords, etc.) usually speak in verse. Prose is more likely to be spoken by servants and other low-status characters.

King Lear contains both verse and prose, but mainly a form of verse called 'blank verse'. About 75 per cent of the play is written in blank verse with the remainder being prose and songs.

Blank Verse

This is a type of poetry that follows these rules:

- Each line has 10 or 11 syllables.
- Each line has five strong beats.

Think of a heart beating: de **DUM** de **DUM** de **DUM** de **DUM** de **DUM**. This is similar to how the beat or stress falls on the syllables in blank verse. In this line, spoken by Kent, the emphasis should fall on the words in **bold**.

De - **Dum** - de - **Dum** - de - **Dum** - de - **Dum** - de - **Dum**

That - **such** - a - **slave** - as - **this** - should - **wear** - a - **sword.**

The lines don't usually rhyme in blank verse, but sometimes major characters are given two lines of rhyming verse to end scenes - particularly at times of crisis - to have a bigger impact. These are called rhyming couplets.

Let me, if not by birth, have lands by wit.
All with me's meet that I can fashion fit.

Edmund, Act 1 Scene 2

No blown ambition doth our arms incite,
But love, dear love, and our aged father's right.

Cordelia, Act 4 Scene 3

A Soliloquy

This is a speech spoken by one character; we're listening to their thoughts.

They are thinking out loud to themselves, or speaking directly to the audience, not to another character (in the graphic novel, we have put some of these in "thought bubbles").

Edmund and Edgar have several soliloquies throughout the play where they reveal to the audience what they are planning and what they really think about the other characters.

Fun Facts

And They All Lived Happily Ever After

The Anglo-Irish poet, Nahum Tate, adapted *King Lear* and rewrote the ending of the play in 1681, claiming that the play needed to be improved and made more believable! He added a romance between Cordelia and Edgar, cut the character of the Fool and gave the tragedy a happy ending. Lear regains his throne and Cordelia survives and marries Edgar.

Many critics thought this was a better play, as the ending of the original was too terrible for the stage. It was the version most performed on the English stage until around 1838.

Where's the Music?

King Lear has been the inspiration for several operas, but there is one famous composer who struggled to produce any music for an operatic version of the play. Giuseppe Verdi, the renowned Italian composer, originally began working on producing music for an operatic libretto of *King Lear* in 1850. However, by the time of the composer's death in 1901, no music for the opera had been composed!

Banned!

During his time on the British throne, King George III suffered from bouts of "insanity". So, all versions of *King Lear* on the English stage were banned between 1810 and 1820, when Shakespeare's fictional king and his mental illness mirrored King George's real-life situation far too closely.

TV and Lear

King Lear continues to inspire modern writers, artists and directors. There have been many films based on the play. One of the most famous is by the Japanese director, Akira Kurosawa. His 1985 film epic, *Ran*, combined *King Lear* with the legend of a Japanese feudal lord.

Two hit TV series were also much influenced by the play. *Empire* follows the story of a hip-hop producer and his three sons' efforts to take over his business. *Succession* follows the Roy family. Brian Cox stars as media-mogul, Logan Roy (the Lear figure) and the series explores the struggles of the family to take over the business, as the father's health fades.

Publication

Shakespeare's plays weren't printed or written as complete plays before they were first performed. Each actor was given their part on a scroll. They had to learn their lines from this. The "Platt" or plot of the play was a list of the scenes with the exits and entrances. This was posted backstage for the actors to follow.

The History of the life and death of King Lear and his three Daughters, was first published in a Quarto edition (see page 106) in 1606. This was probably based on Shakespeare's own working manuscript. It includes over 300 lines *not* included in *The First Folio* edition in 1623. The Folio also has around 100 lines that are not in the Quarto. The Folio edition even changed the title to *The Tragedy of King Lear* and includes many changes to punctuation and to which character speaks various lines.

Modern directors of the play sometimes use a mixture of the Quarto and Folio editions. This graphic adaptation is based on the Folio edition.

Book Fact

There were three main sizes of books in Shakespeare's time.

Folio

A book made from sheets of paper that are folded once to make four pages from one sheet.

Quarto

A smaller book. The sheets of paper are folded twice to make eight pages from one sheet.

Octavo

An even smaller book! The sheets of paper are folded four times to make 16 pages from one sheet.

Performing the Play!

In Shakespeare's time, drama performance and theatre spaces were developing in various ways across the globe. England was no exception.

When Shakespeare began his acting career, there were very few theatres in London.

Plays were performed in inn yards and in the halls and houses of the monarch or wealthy people. But, by the end of Shakespeare's life, plays were being performed in purpose-built theatres across London, where performances took place every day (except Sundays), all year round.

The first purpose-built London playhouse appeared in 1576 when James Burbage, father of Shakespeare's friend, Richard Burbage, constructed a building for performing plays. He called it The Theatre! The success of this space led to other playhouses being built across London.

Key

*Purpose-built theatres

**Inns used for performances

***Indoor theatres

Deadly Serious Fact

Bubonic plague or The Black Death was a big part of Shakespeare's world. Thousands of people died from the plague across the globe.

It is thought to have been passed on by rat fleas which carried deadly bacteria. If you caught the plague, there was a fifty-fifty chance of survival. Whenever there was an outbreak of plague in London, the theatres were shut down, which meant no money for playwrights or actors.

The Theatre

A trip to the theatre to see a play in Shakespeare's time was very different from today. People didn't sit still. They stood, walked around, shouted and chatted to each other. The audience could buy ale, wine, pies, fruit, tobacco and nuts, all while the play was being performed. The audience got as close to the action as possible, so they could hear the actors – there were no microphones in Shakespeare's day!

The plays were aimed at all levels of society – from Lords and Ladies of the court down to tradespeople and commoners. Criminals also visited the playhouses, ready to pick the pockets of unsuspecting members of the audience.

Depending on how rich (and important) you were, you could choose where to sit.

In 1594, a worker's pay was about 8 pence a day, so it meant that plays were affordable to a lot of London's population and therefore many people went to the theatre. The large theatres, such as The Globe, could hold up to 3,000 spectators, including 1,000 groundlings (see opposite).

For indoor playhouses, it was more expensive and therefore the audience members were wealthier.

The Globe Theatre was built in 1599.

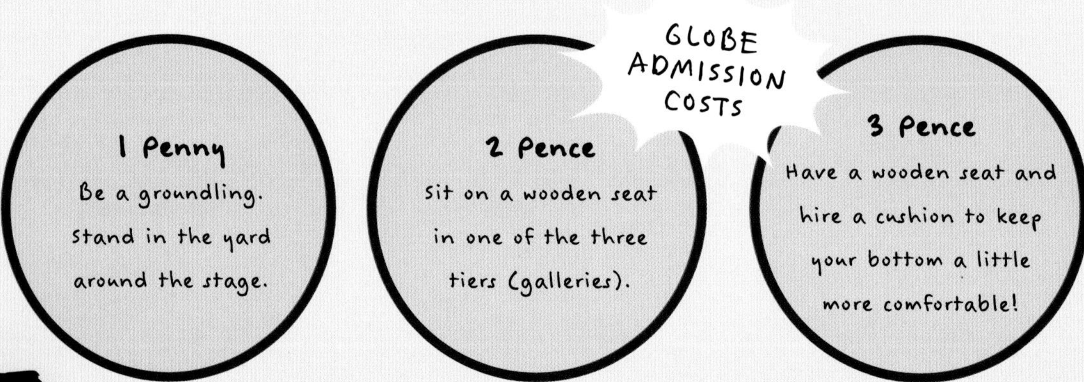

The Globe Theatre

Open-air Playhouse

There would be a different show every afternoon. Coloured flags were used to advertise what play was being put on that day.

Red – History

Black – Tragedy

White – Comedy

Thatched roof

Galleries

Standing area groundlings

Stage (Under stage and above stage used for special effects, storing costumes and changing rooms for actors)

6 Pence
Sit in the Lord's Gallery – rooms on either side of the balcony at the back of the stage.

12 Pence
(1 shilling) sit on the stage.

30 Pence
(2 shillings & 6 pence – or half a crown) you could sit in a private box.

Glossary

The World of Shakespeare's Words

Early Modern English Language was only about 100 years old when Shakespeare started writing in the 16th century. Because Shakespeare often wrote in verse, in order to fit the words into the necessary rhythm, some of the sentence order seems odd to us today:

Cordelia (Early Modern English): Unhappy that I am, I cannot heave
My heart into my mouth.

Cordelia (modern English): I am unlucky, for I cannot put my heart's feelings into words.

Because Shakespeare was writing over 400 years ago, some of the words and phrases he uses can look a bit strange. Some are so old, we don't use them any more at all!

Thou, thee, thy and thine

Shakespeare uses these words A LOT. But they aren't as confusing as they seem!

thou	means	**you**
thee	means	**you**
thy	means	**your**
thine	means	**your**

Sometimes two words are put together. Watch out for the apostrophe!

'twas	means	**it was**
'twere	means	**it were**
'tis	means	**it is**
is't	means	**is it**

Sometimes words have extra letters. Take off the **t** or **st** and see what's left!

hast	means	**has**
wilt	means	**will**
dost	means	**does**
thinkst	means	**think**
hath	means	**has**
didst	means	**did**

Some more old words:

art	means	**are**
ere	means	**before**
forfeit	means	**penalty**
forsaken	means	**abandoned**
hence	means	**from here**
hie	means	**go (hurry)**
wherefore	means	**why**
ye	means	**you**
yonder	means	**there**
fie!	means	**an exclamation of disapproval**

Shakespeare Timeline

We often have no clear information about the dates of Shakespeare's plays. Scholars who study Shakespeare have to rely on information, such as the way each play is put together, the language Shakespeare uses and details in the text that connect to parts of history.

Therefore, the dates of the plays given below are "best guesses" as to the years they were written and first performed.

1558 Queen Mary I dies and her sister, Queen Elizabeth I, takes the throne of England.

1564 Shakespeare is born. Horse-drawn coaches first appear in England.

1567 The first purpose-built theatre in England is built – The Red Lion in Stepney, London.

1576 The Theatre is built in London by James Burbage. 180,000 people now live in London. 300,000 live in Paris, France.

1582 Shakespeare marries Anne Hathaway.

1582 The theatres close down in London due to an outbreak of plague. Thousands of people die.

London's first waterworks is founded.

1583 Susanna (Shakespeare's daughter) is born. (See also 1585)

1584 Ivan The Terrible, first ruler of Russia, dies.

1585 Hamnet and Judith (twins – Shakespeare's son and daughter) are born.

1587 Shakespeare leaves Stratford-upon-Avon and his family for London.

The Rose Theatre is built in London by Philip Henslowe (on Bankside).

Mary Queen of Scots is executed.

1588 The Spanish Armada invade England, but are defeated.

1590/1 Shakespeare's first plays, **THE TWO GENTLEMAN OF VERONA** and **THE TAMING OF THE SHREW**, are performed.

1591 Shakespeare dedicates his poem, *Venus and Adonis*, to the Earl of Southampton. This poem earns him a lot of money!

1592 Shakespeare is mentioned in the press as an up-and-coming playwright.

Plague! All London playhouses are closed for two years.

Many of the acting companies tour the country.

Shakespeare begins writing poems.

The Imjin Wars between Japan and Korea begin.

1593 Playwright and friend of Shakespeare, Christopher Marlowe, is killed in a brawl.

1594 Shakespeare's poem, *The Rape of Lucrece*, is published. Again, it is dedicated to the Earl of Southampton.

1595 Shakespeare becomes a shareholder in The Lord Chamberlain's Men (a very successful and popular acting company).

ROMEO AND JULIET

1596 Shakespeare's son, Hamnet, dies. Shakespeare's father, John, is granted a coat of arms.

England sees its first tomatoes – and its first flushing toilet.

A MIDSUMMER NIGHT'S DREAM

1597 Shakespeare buys New Place in Stratford – one of the largest houses in the town.

Transportation to English colonies is first used as a punishment for criminals.

THE MERCHANT OF VENICE

1598 **MUCH ADO ABOUT NOTHING**

1599 The Globe Theatre is built.

1601 **HAMLET**

TWELFTH NIGHT

Shakespeare's father dies.

1603 Queen Elizabeth dies.

James VI of Scotland takes the throne with the title James I.

Plague hits London. Over 30,000 people die. The theatres are closed again.

The Lord Chamberlain's Men change their name to The King's Men.

They perform at the King's courts and are recognised as the leading theatre company of the time.

1604 The Globe reopens.

1605 The Gunpowder Plot fails to blow up King James and his ministers.

In Spain, Cervantes publishes Part 1 of *Don Quixote*.

1606 **MACBETH**
KING LEAR

Theatres are ordered to close if the weekly number of people who die from the plague rises above 30.
Theatres closed July–December.

1607 Shakespeare's daughter Susanna marries John Hall, a physician in Stratford.

Shakespeare's brother, Edmund (an actor), dies.

Founding of Jamestown, Virginia – first English colony in North America.

1608 Shakespeare's mother, Mary, dies.

Shakespeare becomes a grandfather! Elizabeth is born to Susanna and John Hall.

The King's Men begin to perform at an indoor theatre at Blackfriars.

The telescope is invented by a Dutch scientist and used by Galileo.

1609 Shakespeare's *Sonnets* are published.

The Blue Mosque is built in Constantinople (now Istanbul).

1610 Shakespeare spends more time in Stratford.

1611 **THE TEMPEST**

1612 Shakespeare's brother, Gilbert, dies.

The decimal point is first used by German mathematician Pitiscus.

The Dutch establish a trading post on Manhattan Island (later New York).

1613 The Globe Theatre burns down during a performance of *Henry VIII*.

Shakespeare buys a house in Blackfriars, London.

1614 The Globe Theatre is rebuilt.

1616 Shakespeare's daughter, Judith, marries Thomas Quiney, a Stratford wine merchant.

Shakespeare dies.

1623 Shakespeare's plays are published. *The First Folio* contains 36 of his plays.